Reflections

SERIES

The United States:
MAKING A NEW NATION

Homework and Practice Book
Teacher Edition

Grade 5

SCHOOL PUBLISHERS

Orlando   Austin   New York   San Diego   Toronto   London

Visit *The Learning Site!*
www.harcourtschool.com

Printed in the United States of America

ISBN 0-15-341487-1

6 7 8 9 10   1421   14 13 12 11 10

4500244843

Reflections

CALIFORNIA
SERIES

Contents

This book provides the answers to the activities in the Homework and Practice Book, Student Edition. The table of contents below is organized into three columns. The first column lists the page numbers in this Teacher Edition. The second column identifies the Lesson, Skill, or Review activities shown on each page. The third column correlates the page content to pages in the Homework and Practice Book, Student Edition.

UNIT 1: THE FIRST AMERICANS

UNIT 2: CULTURES MEET

UNIT 3: SETTLING THE COLONIES

UNIT 4: THE AMERICAN REVOLUTION

Chapter 8: The Colonies Unite

Chapter 9: The Revolutionary War

UNIT 5: GOVERNING THE NATION

Chapter 10: The Constitution

Chapter 11: The American Republic

UNIT 6: WESTERN EXPANSION

Chapter 12: The Changing Frontier

Chapter 13: Moving West

Name _____ Date _____

Skills: Use Latitude and Longitude

DIRECTIONS Use the map to find each latitude and longitude given below, and then write the name of the state in each location.

United States Latitude and Longitude

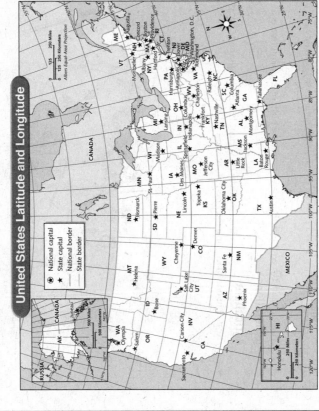

1 30°N, 100°W _____ **Texas**

2 40°N, 90°W _____ **Illinois**

3 40°N, 80°W _____ **Pennsylvania**

4 40°N, 110°W _____ **Utah**

5 30°N, 90°W _____ **Louisiana**

CALIFORNIA STANDARDS HSS 5.9; CS 4

Use after reading Chapter 1, Skill Lesson, pages 22–23.

(continued)

Name _____ Date _____

The Land and States

DIRECTIONS Read each list of three states. Use the map to find a fourth state that borders all three. Write the name of the state and its capital.

The United States

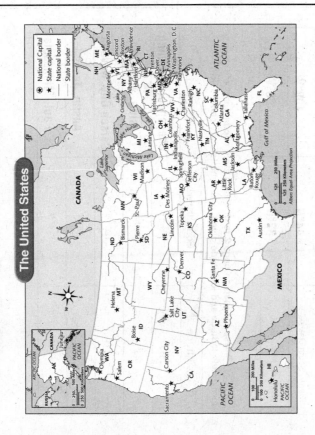

1 Massachusetts, Vermont, Pennsylvania _____ **New Hampshire** , **Concord**

2 Indiana, Michigan, Pennsylvania _____ **Ohio** , **Columbus**

3 Mississippi, Florida, Georgia _____ **Alabama** , **Montgomery**

4 Oregon, Nevada, Arizona _____ **California** , **Sacramento**

5 Arizona, Nevada, Idaho _____ **Utah** , **Salt Lake City**

CALIFORNIA STANDARDS HSS 5.9; CS 4

Use after reading Chapter 1, Lesson 1, pages 14–21.

Name _____ Date _____

DIRECTIONS Describe the absolute location of each state capital. Use the map on page 2 to find the approximate latitude and longitude for each capital listed, and complete the chart below.

State Capital	Latitude	Longitude
Denver, Colorado	40°N	105°W
Trenton, New Jersey	40°N	75°W
Salem, Oregon	45°N	123°W
Pierre, South Dakota	44°N	100°W
Jackson, Mississippi	32°N	90°W

DIRECTIONS Use the map on page 2 to find each state capital for the approximate latitude and longitude given, and complete the chart below.

Latitude	Longitude	State Capital
41°N	105°W	Cheyenne, Wyoming
43°N	85°W	Lansing, Michigan
39°N	120°W	Carson City, Nevada
30°N	98°W	Austin, Texas
45°N	93°W	St. Paul, Minnesota

Use after reading Chapter 1, Skill Lesson, pages 22–23. Homework and Practice Book ■ 3

© Harcourt

Name _____ Date _____

Ancient Indians

DIRECTIONS Fill in the blanks in the sentences below, using terms from the Word Bank.

agriculture	ancestors	generation	legend	theory

1. The Ancient Indians are thought to be the __ancestors__ of present-day American Indians.

2. A story that is handed down from the past is called a __legend__.

3. A __theory__ is a possible explanation that is based on study and research.

4. The average time between the birth of parents and the birth of their children is a __generation__.

5. __Agriculture__ changed the lives of Ancient Indians by giving them a reason to stay in one place for longer periods of time.

CALIFORNIA STANDARDS HSS 5.1, 5.1.2; CS 2

Use after reading Chapter 1, Lesson 2, pages 24–31.

4 ■ Homework and Practice Book

(continued)

© Harcourt

Name _____

Date _____

Skills: Read Time Lines

DIRECTIONS The time line on this page shows events that happened in the Americas. Study the time line, and then complete the statements below.

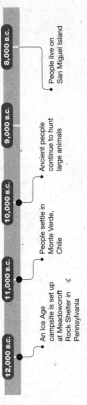

| 12,000 B.C. | 11,000 B.C. | 10,000 B.C. | 9,000 B.C. | 8,000 B.C. |

An Ice Age campsite is set up at Meadowcroft Rock Shelter in Pennsylvania

People settle in Monte Verde, Chile

Ancient people continue to hunt large animals

People live on San Miguel Island

1. Artifacts found in Monte Verde, Chile, provide proof that people were there as long ago as ___11,000 B.C.___

2. Artifacts found at the Meadowcroft Rock Shelter suggest that people were living there in ___12,000 B.C.___

3. By 8,000 B.C., people who used boats were living on ___San Miguel Island___

4. What is the earliest event described on the time line? ___Ancient people camp at Meadowcroft Rock Shelter in Pennsylvania___

5. How many years after people camped at Meadowcroft Rock Shelter did Ancient Indians settle in Monte Verde, Chile? ___1,000 years___

CALIFORNIA STANDARDS HSS 5.1, 5.1.1; CS 1   Use after reading Chapter 1, Skill Lesson, pages 32–33.

Name _____

Date _____

DIRECTIONS Read each statement about the arrival of ancient people in the Americas. In the spaces provided, write *LB* for each statement that refers to the land bridge theory. Write *OT* for each statement that refers to other arrival theories. Write *OS* for each statement that refers to origin stories.

OS 1. Many American Indians believe that their ancestors have always lived in the Americas.

LB 2. Many scientists believe that thousands of years ago, groups of hunters migrated from Asia to North America.

OT 3. Recent discoveries support the idea that ancient peoples came by boat to the Americas.

OS 4. According to the Huron, land was formed from soil found in a turtle's claws.

LB 5. Beringia was named for the Bering Strait, which separates Russia from Alaska.

OT 6. At Meadowcroft Rock Shelter, archaeologists discovered stone tools that may be 14,000 years old.

OS 7. The Blackfoot people tell a story of Old Man the Creator.

LB 8. After hundreds of years, people traveling from Asia reached what is today Alaska.

OT 9. In Monte Verde, Chile, archaeologists uncovered huts, digging sticks, and a child's footprint that may have been there for 13,000 years.

LB 10. At different times, the level of the oceans dropped, causing dry land to appear between Asia and North America.

Use after reading Chapter 1, Lesson 2, pages 24–31.

Name _____ Date _____

Early Civilizations

DIRECTIONS Write *T* or *F* in the blank before each statement to tell whether it is TRUE or FALSE. Rewrite each FALSE statement to make it true.

T **1** The Olmec civilization was one of the earliest in the Americas.

T **2** The Olmec had a calendar to keep track of the seasons.

F **3** The Maya were the first Americans to have a counting system.
The Olmec were the first Americans to have a counting system.

F **4** When the Mayan civilization fell, Mayan culture disappeared.
When the Mayan civilization fell, Mayan culture continued.

T **5** The Hopewell had trade paths from the Rocky Mountains to Lake Superior.

F **6** The people of the Mississippian civilization built pyramids that served as temples.
The people of the Mississippian civilization built mounds that served as temples.

T **7** Cahokia was built by the Mississippians in present-day Illinois.

T **8** The Adena built mounds that were up to 90 feet high.

F **9** The Ancient Puebloans got most of their food by hunting.
The Ancient Puebloans got most of their food by farming.

F **10** The Ancient Puebloans most likely left their land because of attacks by neighboring peoples.
They most likely left their land because of drought.

CALIFORNIA STANDARDS HSS 5.1, 5.1.1, 5.1.2, 5.1.3; HI 2   Homework and Practice Book ■ 7

Use after reading Chapter 1, Lesson 3, pages 36–41.

© Harcourt

Name _____ Date _____

Skills: Use a Cultural Map

DIRECTIONS Use the map to answer the questions on page 9.

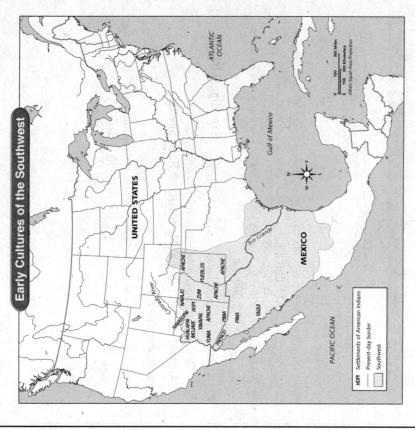

Early Cultures of the Southwest

CALIFORNIA STANDARDS HSS 5.1.1; CS 4; HI 2   Use after reading Chapter 1, Skill Lesson, pages 42–43.

(continued)

© Harcourt

Name _____ Date _____

Study Guide

Chapter 1

DIRECTIONS Fill in the missing information in these paragraphs about the geography and early peoples of the Americas. Use the terms listed below to help you complete the paragraph for each lesson.

Lesson 1	Lesson 2	Lesson 3
Appalachian Mountains	migration	traditions
Great Basin	artifacts	pueblos
Coastal Plain	legends	government
Rocky Mountains	nomads	Cahokia
Interior Plains	Beringia	hieroglyphs

Lesson 1 The United States has a variety of landform regions. The **Coastal Plain** stretches along the East Coast from Massachusetts to Florida. It continues west along the Gulf of Mexico. The **Appalachian Mountains** are the oldest mountains in North America. The **Interior Plains** cover much of the middle of the United States. Farther west is the nation's largest mountain range, the **Rocky Mountains** . In the Intermountain region, the **Great Basin** covers parts of six states.

10 ■ Homework and Practice Book

CALIFORNIA STANDARDS HSS 5.1, 5.1.1, 5.1.2, 5.1.3; HI 2   Use after reading Chapter 1, pages 14–43.

(continued)

Name _____ Date _____

1 Which peoples lived in present-day Mexico?
the Papaco, Pima, and Yaqui

2 Which peoples lived closest to the Colorado River? **the Havasupai, the Hualapai, the Mojave, the Yuma, and the Papaco**

3 Which people lived along a coast?
the Papaco and the Yaqui

4 Which people lived the farthest east?
the Apache

5 Which people lived the farthest south?
the Yaqui

6 What river flows through Apache lands?
the Rio Grande

7 Which people had the most widespread settlements?
the Apache

8 Why do you think the Navajo learned certain customs from the Hopi rather than from the Pima?
because the Navajo lived near the Hopi and not near the Pima

9 Which people lived closest to the mouth of the Colorado River?
the Papaco

10 Which people lived in parts of present-day Mexico and the United States?
the Pima

Use after reading Chapter 1, Skill Lesson, pages 42–43.   Homework and Practice Book ■ 9

READING SOCIAL STUDIES: COMPARE AND CONTRAST

⭐FOCUS Skill Early Civilizations

DIRECTIONS Complete the graphic organizers below to show that you can compare and contrast early civilizations in North America.

Topic 1

Olmec
lasted from 1500 B.C. to A.D. 300; built trade network that used rivers; called "mother culture" of the Americas

Similar
Possible response: ruled southern Mexico; developed calendars; developed a counting system

Topic 2

Maya
lasted from A.D. 300 to A.D. 900; ruled parts of Guatemala and Belize; had social classes

Topic 1

Mound Builders
Possible responses: lived in what is now the central part of the United States; about 30,000 people lived in the city of Cahokia; built mounds made of earth

Similar
Both developed civilizations.

Topic 2

Olmec
Possible responses: ruled most of what is now southern Mexico; built cities, such as San Lorenzo, near rivers; carved large stone heads

CALIFORNIA STANDARDS HSS 5.1, 5.1.1, 5.1.2, 5.1.3

Use after reading Chapter 1, pages 14–43.

Lesson 2   Archaeologists have different theories about how people first came to the Americas. According to one theory, groups of hunters from Asia walked across a land bridge called **Beringia**. Scientists think that this **migration** took place very slowly. Another theory says that people came to the Americas by boat. This theory is supported by fish hooks and other **artifacts** that archaeologists have found on San Miguel Island. Most scientists agree that early Americans most likely were **nomads** who followed animal herds from place to place.

American Indian groups tell **legends** about the distant past. According to these stories, their ancestors have always lived in the Americas.

Lesson 3   Farming led to the first civilizations—advanced cultures that have religion and **government**. The later Maya civilization borrowed many Olmec **traditions**. The Maya civilization also developed a writing system based on **hieroglyphs**. In North America, the Mississippian civilization built the city of **Cahokia**. The city had large mounds used as homes, temples, and burial sites. In the Four Corners area, early civilizations built homes called **pueblos**.

Use after reading Chapter 1, pages 14–43.

Name _____ Date _____

The Desert Southwest

DIRECTIONS Fill in the blanks in the sentences below, using terms from the Word Bank.

adapt	adobe	division of labor	staple	surplus

1. The American Indians of the desert Southwest had to **adapt** their lifeways to meet the challenges of the environment.

2. Maize, beans, and squash were the **staple** _____ foods of the Pueblo Indians.

3. Pueblo Indians built houses from **adobe** _____, which could be made of clay mixed with straw.

4. Having a **surplus** _____ of food meant survival to the people of the desert Southwest in times of drought.

5. The **division of labor** _____ in Hopi society meant that important jobs were divided between men and women.

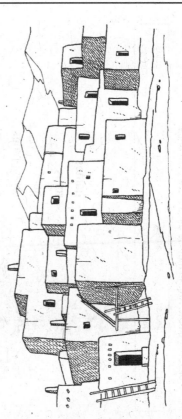

CALIFORNIA STANDARDS HSS 5.1, 5.1.1, 5.1.2, 5.1.3; HI 2

Use after reading Chapter 2, Lesson 1, pages 52–58.

(continued)

Name _____ Date _____

DIRECTIONS Read the facts listed below the chart. Then write the number of each fact in the correct column of the chart.

Hopi	Navajo
2	1
3	4
7	5
8	6
10	9

1. called themselves *Diné*, meaning "The People"
2. lived in pueblos
3. ancestors were the Ancient Puebloans
4. families often lived far from one another
5. lived in hogans
6. called their gods the Holy People
7. well known for their pottery making
8. taught other groups how to farm
9. used sandpaintings in ceremonies
10. lived in villages, usually led by a chief

DIRECTIONS Choose one of the groups shown on the chart above. Write a paragraph about the group and its customs on a separate sheet of paper. Use the chart to help you write your paragraph. You may also include facts that are not on the chart.

Use after reading Chapter 2, Lesson 1, pages 52–58.

Name _____ Date _____

The Plains

DIRECTIONS Read the labels above the boxes. Draw a picture of each item.

Lodge	Tepee

Travois	Sod

DIRECTIONS Choose one of the items you drew. Write a sentence or two describing how the item was made or used. Accept all reasonable answers.

_____

_____

_____

CALIFORNIA STANDARDS HSS 5.1, 5.1.1; HI 2   Use after reading Chapter 2, Lesson 3, pages 68–73.

16 ■ Homework and Practice Book

© Harcourt

Name _____ Date _____

The Pacific Northwest

DIRECTIONS Use the Word Bank to identify the uses of the natural resources in the pictures below. A term may be used more than once.

homes	tools	boats	food	totem poles
water	fish	transportation	masks	oil for lamps

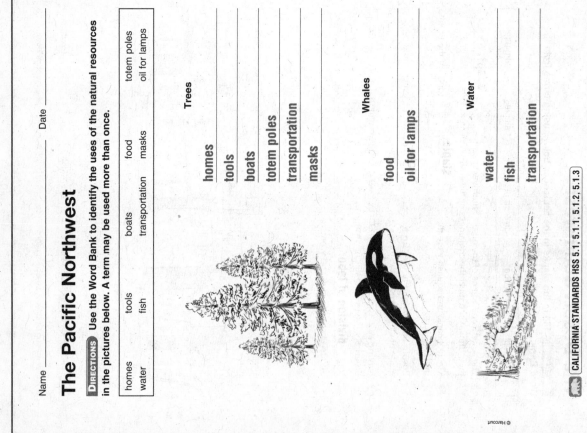

Trees

homes _____

tools _____

boats _____

totem poles _____

transportation _____

masks _____

Whales

food _____

oil for lamps _____

Water

water _____

fish _____

transportation _____

CALIFORNIA STANDARDS HSS 5.1, 5.1.1, 5.1.2, 5.1.3

Use after reading Chapter 2, Lesson 2, pages 60–65.   Homework and Practice Book ■ 15

© Harcourt

© Harcourt

Name _____ Date _____

The Eastern Woodlands

DIRECTIONS Read the passage. Then answer the questions that follow.

In the late 1500s, Iroquois villages often battled among themselves. Often, these battles grew out of small disputes. According to tradition, a Huron named Deganawida believed that the battles must stop if the Iroquois tribes were to protect their ways of life from European newcomers. Deganawida persuaded a Mohawk leader named Hiawatha to join him in spreading throughout Iroquois country the message that "All shall receive the Great Law and labor together for the welfare of man."

The result of their effort was a confederation called the Iroquois League, made up of the Five Nations of the Seneca, the Cayuga, the Onondaga, the Oneida, and the Mohawk. A few years later, a sixth nation, the Tuscarora, joined the league.

Each nation in the league governed itself, and matters were often settled by unanimous vote. Very important matters, such as war, were left for discussion by a Grand Council of 50 chiefs.

1 Who was Deganawida?
According to tradition, he was a Huron who, with a Mohawk named Hiawatha, convinced the Iroquois tribes that they must stop their battles and work together to protect their ways of life.

2 Why did Deganawida think it was important to stop the fighting?
He believed the Iroquois needed to stop fighting so they could band together to protect their way of life from settlers.

3 What tribes belonged to the Iroquois League?
the Seneca, the Cayuga, the Onondaga, the Oneida, the Mohawk, and, later, the Tuscarora

4 How did the Iroquois League make decisions that affected all its nations?
Important issues were decided by a Grand Council of 50 chiefs.

5 What do you think Deganawida meant when he said, "All shall receive the Great Law and labor together for the welfare of man"?
He meant that if the nations joined together and worked for the common good, all Iroquois would benefit.

CALIFORNIA STANDARDS HSS 5.1, 5.1.3; HI 2

Use after reading Chapter 2, Lesson 4, pages 74–79.

Homework and Practice Book ■ 17

© Harcourt

Name _____ Date _____

Skills: Resolve Conflict

DIRECTIONS Complete the graphic organizer below. For each step, write the decisions that led to the formation of the Iroquois League.

Identify the Problem

1 Answers should reflect that fighting among the Iroquois prevented them from protecting their ways of life from European newcomers.

↓

All Sides Clearly State Wants and Needs

2 Each tribe had competing wants and needs for resources such as land, which prevented them from achieving lasting peace.

↓

All Sides Decide What is Most Important

3 Answers should reflect that the Five Nations agreed that lasting peace was vital if they were to preserve their lifeways.

↓

All Sides Plan and Discuss Possible Compromises

4 Accept all answers indicating that a new governing body was needed to resolve disputes while working toward the common good.

↓

All Sides Plan a Lasting Compromise

5 Answers should include the setup of the Iroquois League and the power of the Grand Council to decide matters.

CALIFORNIA STANDARDS HSS 5.1, 5.1.3

18 ■ Homework and Practice Book

Use after reading Chapter 2, Skill Lesson, pages 80–81.

Skills: Use Tables to Group Information

DIRECTIONS Fill in the blanks to complete the table.

Table A: Tribes and Their Staple Foods

Tribe	Climate and Geography	Staple Foods
Hopi	hot, dry desert	corn, beans, squash
Makah	rainy coastal area	salmon, whales
Cheyenne	dry, flat plains	buffalo
Iroquois	moderate climate, forest	corn, beans, squash
Inuit	extremely cold, harsh land	seals

CALIFORNIA STANDARDS HSS 5.1, 5.1.1; HI 2   Use after reading Chapter 2, Skill Lesson, pages 88–89.

(continued)

© Harcourt

The Arctic

DIRECTIONS Read each question below, and choose the best answer. Then fill in the circle for the answer you have chosen.

1 What did Arctic peoples most often use to build their homes?
- (A) stones
- (B) wood
- (C) adobe
- (D) ice

2 What did Arctic peoples most often use to make tools?
- (A) iron
- (B) bones
- (C) wood
- (D) stones

3 How did Arctic peoples get most of their food?
- (A) by hunting
- (B) by farming
- (C) by trading
- (D) by gathering

4 What did Arctic peoples use as fuel for fires?
- (A) wood
- (B) sod
- (C) seal blubber
- (D) buffalo chips

5 Which of the following was NOT hunted by Arctic peoples?
- (A) caribou
- (B) foxes
- (C) seals
- (D) buffalo

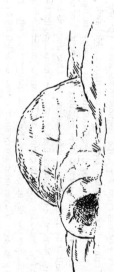

CALIFORNIA STANDARDS HSS 5.1, 5.1.1

© Harcourt

Name _____ Date _____

Chapter 2 Study Guide

DIRECTIONS Fill in the missing information in these paragraphs about American Indians. Use the terms listed below to help you complete the paragraph for each lesson.

Lesson 1	Lesson 2	Lesson 3	Lesson 4	Lesson 5
surplus	bartered	council	confederation	kayaks
ceremonies	clan	tepees	Iroquois	harpoons
adobe	potlatch	sod	Algonquians	igloos

Lesson 1 The peoples of the desert Southwest had to adapt to a land with extreme temperatures and little water. They planted their crops at the bottoms of mesas, where they could catch rainwater. They used stones and mud or **adobe** to build pueblos. They stored **surplus** corn to eat when food was scarce. To bring good harvests, they held **ceremonies** that lasted several days.

Lesson 2 In the Pacific Northwest all the members of a **clan** often lived together in a longhouse. The various groups in the region formed large trade networks. People **bartered** for goods at trading centers such as The Dalles. People from dozens of tribes, some speaking very different languages, traveled hundreds of miles to trade there. Wealthy people showed their wealth by giving a celebration called a **potlatch**. This celebration might last up to ten days and include dancing, food, and speeches.

CALIFORNIA STANDARDS HSS 5.1, 5.1.1, 5.1.2, 5.1.3

22 ■ Homework and Practice Book Use after reading Chapter 2, pages 52–89.

(continued)

Name _____ Date _____

DIRECTIONS Complete the table below. Use the information from the table on page 20, but group the information in a new way.

Table B: Staple Foods by Tribe

Staple Foods	Climate and Geography	Tribe
corn, beans, squash	hot, dry desert; moderate climate, forest	Hopi; Iroquois
salmon, whales	rainy coastal area	Makah
buffalo	dry, flat plains	Cheyenne
seals	extremely cold, harsh land	Inuit

DIRECTIONS Use the information in both tables to answer the questions below.

1. Which table makes it easier to find out what the climate is like where an American Indian tribe lives? **Table A**

2. What table would you use if you wanted to find out what staple foods can be found in different climates? **Table B**

3. Which table makes it easier to find out which staple foods American Indian tribes had in common? **Table B**

READING SOCIAL STUDIES: COMPARE AND CONTRAST

⭐ American Indians

DIRECTIONS Complete this graphic organizer to show that you can compare and contrast the American Indians who lived in different regions of North America.

Topic 1

Pacific Northwest People

used whales for food and oil; made totem poles

Similar

Possible response: used trees to meet many of their needs; hunted, fished, and gathered food; lived in longhouses

Topic 2

Eastern Woodlands People

some groups grew crops; used wampum

Topic 1

The Arctic People

Possible response: lived in very cold surroundings; lived in a region that was too cold to farm; hunted and shared food to survive

Similar

They adapted their way of life to a harsh environment.

Topic 2

The People of the Desert Southwest

Possible response: lived in a dry land of intense heat and bitter cold; grew crops at the bottoms of mesas, where they could catch rainwater; stored surplus food to survive times of drought

CALIFORNIA STANDARDS HSS 5.1, 5.1.1, 5.1.2, 5.1.3

Use after reading Chapter 2, pages 52–89.

Lesson 3 Plains Indians had varied ways of life. In areas where grass was plentiful, some people built lodges covered with **sod**. Other groups used buffalo skins to make tents called **tepees**. Among the Lakota, each group governed itself. The Cheyenne leaders gathered as a **council** to make decisions that all Cheyenne followed. The buffalo was the main source of food for all the American Indian groups that lived on the Great Plains.

Lesson 4 The **Iroquois** lived in the northeastern part of the Eastern Woodlands, around the Great Lakes. They grew crops, and they also hunted and fished. In the 1500s, they formed a **confederation** to settle their disputes and to defend themselves. The **Algonquians** lived farther east, on the Coastal Plain. Because of the plentiful supply of fish near the coast, these tribes relied less on growing crops.

Lesson 5 The peoples of the Arctic region adapted to a frozen, barren land. At times, they used ice to build homes called **igloos**. From animal skins, they made **kayaks** that they paddled on the sea. They used **harpoons** to hunt seals and other animals that they depended on to meet most of their needs. These ways helped the peoples of the Arctic region adapt to and survive in harsh surroundings.

Use after reading Chapter 2, pages 52–89.

Name _____ Date _____

Exploration and Technology

DIRECTIONS Fill in the missing words in this letter from Christopher Columbus to Queen Isabella. Use the terms in the Word Bank.

technology
expedition
benefits
empire
costs

Dear Queen Isabella,

Thank you for agreeing to pay for my **expedition** . With an improved compass and astrolabe, I am sure that I have the **technology** I need to reach Asia. As you know, the **costs** of the journey are high. But I assure you, the **benefits** also will be great. Your **empire** will gain great wealth and vast lands.

Your servant,

Christopher Columbus

CALIFORNIA STANDARDS HSS 5.2, 5.2.1

Use after reading Chapter 3, Lesson 1, pages 110–117. Homework and Practice Book ■ **25**

Name _____ Date _____

A Changing World

DIRECTIONS Read each statement about the aims, obstacles, and accomplishments of the explorers listed below. In the space provided, write the name of the explorer who would have been most likely to have made the statement.

Balboa	Caboto	Magellan	Vespucci

1. "I sailed to a place south of where Columbus had landed, but the coast I traveled along did not match Polo's descriptions of Asia."
   Vespucci

2. "I led the first European expedition to reach the Pacific Ocean."
   Balboa

3. "It took us more than three months to cross the Pacific Ocean, and many among my crew died of hunger and illness."
   Magellan

4. "The English king sent me on an expedition to the Indies, to help England compete for land and wealth."
   Caboto

5. "I was the first explorer of my time to actually set foot in Asia."
   Magellan

6. "A German mapmaker named a continent after me."
   Vespucci

7. "I was looking for gold on an isthmus, but I found something else that was just as important."
   Balboa

8. "I led the first expedition that sailed around the world."
   Magellan

9. "When I reached what I thought was China, I saw many white bears and very large stags that looked like horses."
   Caboto

10. "I did not find the large cities or the wealthy rulers of Asia that I had read about in books."
    Vespucci

CALIFORNIA STANDARDS HSS 5.2, 5.2.2

26 ■ Homework and Practice Book   Use after reading Chapter 3, Lesson 2, pages 120–125.

© Harcourt

Skills: Distinguish Fact from Opinion

DIRECTIONS Read each statement below. In the space provided, write *F* if the statement is a fact. Write *O* if the statement is an opinion.

1 **O** Juan Ponce de León was foolish if he thought that he would find the Fountain of Youth.

2 **F** Juan Ponce de León may have heard that there was a Fountain of Youth on Bimini.

3 **F** Hernando Cortés wanted the Aztecs' gold.

4 **O** I think that Hernando Cortés was a good leader.

5 **O** Hernando Cortés was a terrible man for conquering the Aztecs.

6 **F** Juan Ponce de León was the first Spanish explorer to visit what is now the United States.

DIRECTIONS Write one fact and one opinion about each conquistador named below.

Francisco Vásquez de Coronado

7 Fact: **Possible response: Coronado was looking for a golden city.**

8 Opinion: **Possible response: I think it is sad that Coronado failed** to find the city.

Hernando de Soto

9 Fact: **Possible response: De Soto hoped to find gold.**

10 Opinion: **Possible response: De Soto was a terrible leader because he failed to find gold.**

CALIFORNIA STANDARDS HSS 5.2, 5.2.1, 5.2.2   Use after reading Chapter 3, Skill Lesson, pages 136–137.

28 ■ Homework and Practice Book

© Harcourt

Spanish Explorations

DIRECTIONS Use the map to answer the questions that follow about the routes of Spanish explorers and the distances they traveled.

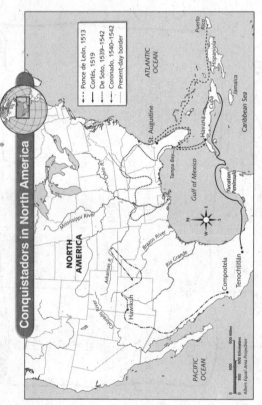

Conquistadors in North America

Map legend:
- ◦◦◦ Ponce de León, 1513
- — Cortés, 1519
- ▪▪▪ De Soto, 1539–1542
- --- Coronado, 1540–1542
- –··– Present-day border

1 Which conquistador traveled the longest distance on land? **Coronado**

2 Which conquistador crossed the Mississippi River? **De Soto**

3 Which conquistadors reached the Arkansas River? **De Soto and Coronado**

4 Which conquistador traveled the farthest north? **Coronado**

5 Which conquistadors traveled through present-day Mexico? **Cortés and Coronado**

6 Which conquistador started his exploration in Puerto Rico? **Ponce de León**

CALIFORNIA STANDARDS HSS 5.2, 5.2.3; CS 4

Use after reading Chapter 3, Lesson 3, pages 128–134.   Homework and Practice Book ■ 27

© Harcourt

Other Nations Explore

Name _____ Date _____

DIRECTIONS Imagine that you are Giovanni da Verrazano and you are being interviewed by a newspaper reporter. Write answers to the interview questions.

1 Mr. Verrazano, what was the aim of your voyages to the west?

Possible response: I wanted to find the Northwest Passage in order to gain wealth and power for France.

2 Who sent you to find the Northwest Passage?

Possible response: The French king, Francis I, sent me to find the Northwest Passage through North America.

3 What was the biggest obstacle that you faced?

Possible response: I found a long coastline, but I could not find a water route leading to Asia.

4 You did not achieve your goal, but what did you accomplish?

Possible response: I explored hundreds of miles of coastline previously unknown to Europeans, and I met some of the people who live there.

5 What were these people like?

Possible response: They were friendly, but it was hard to communicate with them since, of course, their languages are different from ours.

CALIFORNIA STANDARDS HSS 5.2, 5.2.2

Use after reading Chapter 3, Lesson 4, pages 138–143.　　　Homework and Practice Book ▪ 29

Skills: Use an Elevation Map

Name _____ Date _____

DIRECTIONS Add details to the map as described in each item below.

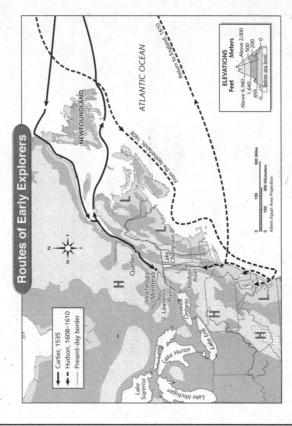

Routes of Early Explorers

→ Cartier, 1535
→ Hudson, 1608–1610
— Present-day border

ATLANTIC OCEAN

NEWFOUNDLAND

From the Netherlands, 1609
Return to England, 1610

Lake Superior
Lake Michigan
Lake Huron
Lake Erie
Lake Ontario
Lake Champlain
Hudson River
St. Lawrence River
Hochelaga (Montreal)
Quebec

ELEVATIONS
Feet　Meters
Above 6,560　Above 2,000
1,640　500
655　200
Below sea level　0

0　150　300 Miles
0　150　300 Kilometers
Albers Equal-Area Projection

1 Write an *H* on any part of the map that shows the highest elevation in the region.
See map for examples of correct placement.

2 Write an *L* on any part of the map that shows the lowest elevation in the region.
See map for examples of correct placement.

CALIFORNIA STANDARDS HSS 5.2; CS 4

30 ▪ Homework and Practice Book　　　Use after reading Chapter 3, Skill Lesson, pages 144–145.

(continued)

Name _____

Date _____

Unit 3

Study Guide

DIRECTIONS Fill in the missing information in these paragraphs about European exploration of the Americas. Use the terms below to help you complete the paragraph for each lesson.

Lesson 1	Lesson 2	Lesson 3	Lesson 4
technology	isthmus	missionaries	St. Lawrence River
benefits	Ferdinand Magellan	grants	mutinied
navigation	Amerigo Vespucci	conquistadors	Northwest Passage
expedition	Newfoundland		
entrepreneur			

Lesson 1   In the 1400s, Europeans entered into a new age of learning, science, and art called the Renaissance. They read about the riches of Asia, but they lacked the knowledge and the tools to reach Asia by sea. To help solve these problems Prince Henry of Portugal started a school to teach ___**navigation**___. People at the school developed new kinds of ___**technology**___, including better compasses and astrolabes. Christopher Columbus led an ___**expedition**___ with the goal of sailing west to Asia. Like other explorers, Columbus was an ___**entrepreneur**___. He persuaded Queen Isabella to pay for his journey by promising her ___**benefits**___ such as riches from Asia.

(continued)

CALIFORNIA STANDARDS HSS 5.2, 5.2.1, 5.2.2, 5.2.3   Use after reading Chapter 3, pages 110–145.

Name _____

Date _____

DIRECTIONS Use the map on page 30 to answer these questions.

3 What is the range of elevation where the city of Montreal is located?

0, or sea level, to 655 feet

4 What is the highest range of elevation to the north of Quebec?

1,640 to 6,560 feet

5 What was the range of elevation for the water route taken by Cartier from Quebec to Montreal?

0, or sea level, to 655 feet

6 How would land elevation have changed if Cartier had traveled 150 miles west from Montreal?

The land elevation would have become higher.

7 How would you describe the land elevation to the east of Hudson's route shown on the Hudson River?

The land elevation might rise a little but it would become flatter near the coast.

8 How would you describe the land elevation to the west of Hudson's route shown on the Hudson River?

The land elevation rises to the west of the Hudson River.

9 What kind of landform would you expect to find at the highest elevations to the west of Hudson's route?

Possible response: hills or mountains

10 Write a sentence describing the land that the Hudson River flows through.

Possible response: The river flows through a hilly land into a broader, lower-lying land.

Use after reading Chapter 3, Skill Lesson, pages 144–145.   Homework and Practice Book ■ 31

Name _____ Date _____

READING SOCIAL STUDIES: MAIN IDEA AND DETAILS

🔶 The Age of Exploration

DIRECTIONS Complete this graphic organizer to show that you understand the main idea and supporting details about European explorations of the Americas.

Main Idea

Europeans explored and claimed lands in the Americas.

Details

Possible response: Columbus sailed west and reached land across the Atlantic.	Possible response: After Columbus's voyages, rulers sent explorers across the Atlantic Ocean to claim new lands.	Possible response: Spanish conquistadors searched for gold and claimed land in the Americas for Spain.	Possible response: Explorers sent by France, England, and Holland explored the east coast of North America in search of both riches and the Northwest Passage.

CALIFORNIA STANDARDS HSS 5.2, 5.2.1, 5.2.2, 5.2.3

Use after reading Chapter 3, pages 110–145.

© Harcourt

Name _____ Date _____

Lesson 2 Other explorers followed Columbus across the Atlantic. Giovanni Caboto sailed west to present-day **Newfoundland**. Caboto thought that he had reached Asia. He knew that Caboto was wrong, though. He realized that Caboto and other explorers had found a continent unknown to Europeans. It was **Amerigo Vespucci**.

It was Vasco Núñez de Balboa who found the key to reaching Asia. He crossed an **isthmus** and saw the Pacific Ocean. **Ferdinand Magellan** was the first European to cross the Pacific Ocean and reach Asia.

Lesson 3 The ruler of Spain wanted explorers to find riches in lands that Spain had claimed. Spain offered **grants** to men who were willing to lead expeditions to the Americas. These men were known as **conquistadors**. The Catholic Church also wanted to extend its power to the Americas. For that reason, it sent **missionaries** to convert American Indians.

Lesson 4 Other explorers still hoped to find a water route to Asia. This route became known as the **Northwest Passage**. Jacques Cartier traveled up the **St. Lawrence River**, hoping that it would lead to Asia. Henry Hudson explored other rivers and bays with the same goal. Hudson failed, and his crew **mutinied** and set him adrift.

Use after reading Chapter 3, pages 110–145.

© Harcourt

The Virginia Colony

DIRECTIONS Complete the organizer to show important facts about the settlers who founded Jamestown.

The Founding of Jamestown

Who	What	When	Where	Why
A group of 105 colonists arrived in Virginia.	They built shelters, planted gardens, and had conflicts with Indians.	1607	They built on low, swampy land along the James River.	They hoped to make money.

DIRECTIONS Using the lines provided, write one fact that tells how each person was important to the survival of the Jamestown settlers.

John Smith

He made it a rule that colonists who did not work did not eat. Soon, colonists were building shelters and growing crops in order to survive.

Pocahontas

According to legend, she saved John Smith from being killed by her father, Chief Powhatan.

John Rolfe

He found a kind of tobacco that proved to be very popular in England. Virginia farmers grew this cash crop on large plantations and made a lot of money.

(continued)

CALIFORNIA STANDARDS HSS 5.2, 5.2.2, 5.4, 5.4.2; HI 2   Use after reading Chapter 4, Lesson 2, pages 160–166.

The Spanish Colonies

DIRECTIONS Read the paragraph. Then answer the questions below.

Santa Fe, New Mexico

In 1598, Juan de Oñate led a large group of people from Mexico north to what would become the Spanish colony of New Mexico. They made the long, difficult journey in search of golden cities. They did not find them, but many people stayed and settled in the area. In 1610, they built a city high on a plateau, where the climate was cooler than it was in the surrounding desert. They named the city Santa Fe, which is Spanish for "holy faith." It was the first permanent European settlement in western North America. In the years after Santa Fe was founded, new settlers and missionaries added to its population. Santa Fe became the capital of Spain's vast territory in New Mexico.

1 Who led the first settlers to New Mexico? **Juan de Oñate**

2 What city was the capital of New Mexico? **Santa Fe**

3 Why did Europeans first travel to New Mexico? **They hoped to find golden cities.**

4 Why did the settlers build their city on a plateau? **because the weather was cooler than in the desert below**

5 When was the first permanent European settlement in western North America built? **in 1610**

CALIFORNIA STANDARDS HSS 5.2.2

Use after reading Chapter 4, Lesson 1, pages 154–158.   **Homework and Practice Book ▪ 35**

Name _____ **Date** _____

© Harcourt

DIRECTIONS Use your completed organizer to help you write a narrative about life in early Jamestown. Your narrative may include facts that are not on the organizer.

John Smith   Pocahontas

Possible response:

In 1607, 105 colonists settled along the James River. They named the settlement Jamestown in honor of the English king, James I. They built it on low, swampy land, which led to problems with mosquitoes and illness. The colonists had come to Virginia hoping to get rich, and many of them did not want to work hard. When John Smith took over as their leader, he made a rule that anyone who did not work did not eat. The colonists began building shelters and planting gardens. Jamestown succeeded even though colonists often had conflicts with Indians.

Use after reading Chapter 4, Lesson 2, pages 160–166.   Homework and Practice Book ▪ 37

Name _____ **Date** _____

Skills: Compare Primary and Secondary Sources

DIRECTIONS Study the photo and illustration below, and use the information they contain to answer questions about primary and secondary sources.

THE NEW LIFE of Virginea: DECLARING THE FORMER SVCCESSE AND PRE- together with the present estate and part of Nova Britannia. Caveat of Virginia. LONDON.

Imprinted by Felix Kingston for William Welby, dwelling at the Signe of the Swan in Pauls Churchyard, 1612.

1 Is the title page of the book shown a primary or a secondary source? How can you tell?
Primary. The year of 1612 is written on the title page of the book. This tells when the book was published.

2 How can you tell that the picture of the Virginia settler is a secondary source?
The picture is a photograph of a historical reenactor.

3 What do the two sources have in common?
They both present information about life in the Virginia Colony.

CALIFORNIA STANDARDS HSS 5.2.2, 5.3; HR 1

38 ▪ Homework and Practice Book   Use after reading Chapter 4, Skill Lesson, pages 168–169.

(continued)

Name _____ Date _____

DIRECTIONS This modern drawing shows what the houses built outside the Jamestown fort may have looked like in the early 1600s. Use it to answer the questions that follow.

4 Why did Jamestown settlers have fields so close to their homes?
Possible response: They were afraid of being attacked by Indians.

5 Is the drawing of Jamestown a primary or a secondary source? Explain why.
Possible response: The drawing is a secondary source because it is a modern drawing. The person who made it did not actually live during the time of the Jamestown Colony.

Use after reading Chapter 4, Skill Lesson, pages 168–169.　　Homework and Practice Book ■ 39

© Harcourt

Name _____ Date _____

The Plymouth Colony

DIRECTIONS When the Mayflower Compact was written in 1620, the English language was very different from what it is today. Below is a version of the Mayflower Compact written in present-day language. Use it to answer the questions that follow.

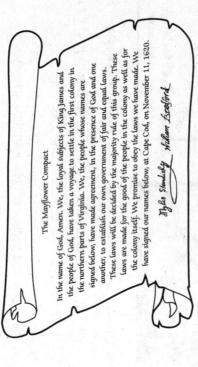

The Mayflower Compact

In the name of God, Amen. We, the loyal subjects of King James and the people of God, have taken a voyage to settle in the first colony in the northern parts of Virginia. We, the people whose names are signed below, have made agreement, in the presence of God and one another, to establish our own government of fair and equal laws. These laws will be decided by the majority rule of this group. These laws are made for the good of the people in the colony as well as for the colony itself. We promise to obey the laws we have made. We have signed our names below, at Cape Cod, on November 11, 1620.

Myles Standish   William Bradford

1 Who is the English ruler named in the Mayflower Compact?
King James

2 Where did the Mayflower passengers think they were going to settle?
in the northern parts of Virginia

3 How did the writers of the Mayflower Compact say laws would be decided?
by majority rule

4 What did the passengers promise?
They promised to obey the laws they made.

5 Where and when was the Mayflower Compact signed?
It was signed at Cape Cod, on November 11, 1620.

CALIFORNIA STANDARDS HSS 5.4, 5.4.5

40 ■ Homework and Practice Book　　Use after reading Chapter 4, Lesson 3, pages 170–175.

© Harcourt

Skills: Read a Historical Map

DIRECTIONS Use the map on this page to help you answer the questions on page 43.

European Claims in the Eastern Part of North America, 1650

CREE
MICMAC
ABENAKI
MAHICAN
Quebec
St. Lawrence River
NEW FRANCE
ALGONKIN
MASSACHUSET
Boston
MA
Plymouth
CT
RI
NEW NETHERLAND
IROQUOIS
New Amsterdam
NEW ENGLAND
NEW SWEDEN
DE
OTTAWA
Lake Ontario
HURON
ERIE
POWHATAN
MD
Jamestown
VA
Sault Ste. Marie
L. Huron
Lake Superior
WINNEBAGO
TUSCARORA
ATLANTIC OCEAN
CHIPPEWA
Lake Michigan
SAUK
FOX
MIAMI
SHAWNEE
CHEROKEE
YAMASEE
St. Augustine
CALUSA
ILLINOIS
Mississippi River
IOWA
MISSOURI
OSAGE
QUAPAW
CADDO
NATCHEZ
CHICKASAW
CHOCTAW
CREEK
BILOXI
Gulf of Mexico
Havana
ARAWAK
ATAKAPA
N W E S

125 250 Miles
125 250 Kilometers
Lambert Equal-Area Projection

French
Spanish
English
Dutch
Swedish
• Major settlements
FOX Name of Native American Tribe
— Present-day border

42 ■ Homework and Practice Book

CALIFORNIA STANDARDS HSS 5.2, 5.2.4; CS 4

Use after reading Chapter 4, Skill Lesson, pages 184–185.

(continued)

The French and the Dutch

DIRECTIONS Read each question below and choose the best answer. Then fill in the circle for the answer you have chosen.

1 Why did French merchants help set up settlements in North America?
   Ⓐ They wanted the Indians' gold.
   Ⓑ They wanted wealth from the fur trade.
   Ⓒ They wanted to control the route to Asia.
   Ⓓ They wanted to force the Spanish off their land.

2 What kept Marquette and Joliet from reaching the mouth of the Mississippi River?
   Ⓐ They got lost.
   Ⓑ They ran out of food.
   Ⓒ They were attacked by Indians.
   Ⓓ They feared meeting Spanish soldiers.

3 Who was the first French explorer to reach the mouth of the Mississippi River?
   Ⓐ Jacques Cartier
   Ⓑ Samuel de Champlain
   Ⓒ Sieur de la Salle
   Ⓓ Pierre Le Moyne

4 What was one problem that early French settlements faced?
   Ⓐ Few French people wanted to settle in North America.
   Ⓑ Indians refused to trade with the French.
   Ⓒ Spanish soldiers attacked French forts.
   Ⓓ Colonies grew quickly, and good land was scarce.

5 What was the aim of Dutch settlers coming to North America?
   Ⓐ to make money by selling furs
   Ⓑ to find good farmland
   Ⓒ to escape war in Europe
   Ⓓ to practice their religion

CALIFORNIA STANDARDS HSS 5.2, 5.2.2

Use after reading Chapter 4, Lesson 4, pages 176–183.

Homework and Practice Book ■ 41

© Harcourt

Name _____ Date _____

1. What time in history does the map show? **1650**

2. What were the major settlements in Spanish areas? **St. Augustine, Havana**

3. What country controlled the St. Lawrence River? **France**

4. What country claimed land where the Powhatan lived? **England**

5. What country claimed land near to where the Huron lived? **France**

6. Who settled the land known as New Netherland? **the Dutch**

7. What American Indian group lived in the southern part of what is now the state of Florida? **the Calusa**

8. Which country's settlements extended farthest north? **England's**

9. Which country claimed the most land? **Spain**

10. Describe the location of Swedish settlements relative to the settlements of New England. **New Sweden was surrounded by English settlements in all four directions.**

© Harcourt

Chapter 4

Name _____ Date _____

Study Guide

DIRECTIONS Fill in the missing information in these paragraphs about the first colonies. Use the terms below to help you complete the paragraph for each lesson.

Lesson 1	Lesson 2	Lesson 3	Lesson 4
haciendas	raw materials	Samoset	New Orleans
presidios	cash crop	Tisquantum	Quebec
plantations	royal colony	William Bradford	New Amsterdam
missions	legislature		
borderlands			

Lesson 1 Some early Spanish settlers hoped to find gold, and others started large farms. However, there was a shortage of workers to do the labor necessary on a large farm. To find the workers they needed, some Spanish settlers enslaved Indians to work on these **plantations**. Spanish soldiers built **presidios** to protect lands on the edge of New Spain. Ranchers built large estates, or **haciendas**, in the outlying lands. Spain did not want to lose these **borderlands** to other countries. The Spanish also built **missions**, where Spanish priests and Indians lived side by side.

CALIFORNIA STANDARDS HSS 5.2, 5.2.2, 5.3, 5.3.1, 5.3.3   Use after reading Chapter 4, pages 154–185.

44 ■ Homework and Practice Book

(continued)

© Harcourt

Name _____ Date _____

Lesson 2 England hoped to profit from ____**raw materials**____, such as lumber, from its Virginia Colony. The colonists themselves made money from tobacco, a ____**cash crop**____ that they sold to England. As the colony grew, it needed laws. The Virginia ____**legislature**____ was the first representative assembly in the English colonies. After the Powhatan Wars, though, King James I took over Virginia, making it a ____**royal colony**____.

Lesson 3 The Pilgrims settled in Massachusetts, where they had religious freedom. They had good leaders, including ____**William Bradford**____, who invited neighboring Indians to share the first harvest. The Indians were helpful to the Pilgrims. An Abenaki Indian named ____**Samoset**____ visited the Pilgrims. He brought a Wampanoag Indian named ____**Tisquantum**____, who taught the settlers how to farm and fish.

Lesson 4 Samuel de Champlain built ____**Quebec**____, the first French settlement in North America. French settlements grew slowly. More than 100 years passed before the city of ____**New Orleans**____ was founded and became the capital of France's southern colony, Louisiana. The Dutch competed with the French for the fur trade. The first Dutch colony was New Netherland, and its main trading center was ____**New Amsterdam**____.

Name _____ Date _____

READING SOCIAL STUDIES: MAIN IDEA AND DETAILS

(Focus Skill)

The First Colonies

DIRECTIONS Complete this graphic organizer to show that you understand the main idea and some supporting details about the first European colonies in the Americas.

Main Idea

Europeans started colonies in North America.

Details

Possible response: The Spanish built plantations, presidios, and missions throughout New Spain to keep control of lands they claimed.	Possible response: English colonists, hoping to get rich, built settlements in Virginia.	Possible response: Another group of English colonists, the Pilgrims, settled in New England, seeking religious freedom and economic opportunities.	Possible response: The Dutch and French started settlements to make money from the fur trade.

CALIFORNIA STANDARDS HSS 5.2, 5.2.2

Settling New England

DIRECTIONS Read each statement below. On the blank provided, write the name of the person whom the statement describes. You may use some names more than once.

Thomas Hooker	Anne Hutchinson	Metacomet
David Thomson	Roger Williams	John Winthrop

1 This person lived with the Narragansett Indians after being expelled from the Massachusetts Colony. __Roger Williams__

2 This person founded a fishing village that became part of the New Hampshire Colony. __David Thomson__

3 This person was a leader of the group that settled Boston. __John Winthrop__

4 This person became a leader in the Connecticut Colony. __Thomas Hooker__

5 This person founded a settlement that later joined with Providence and became part of Rhode Island. __Anne Hutchinson__

6 This person helped write the Fundamental Orders. __Thomas Hooker__

7 This person decided to fight rather than be forced from his land. __Metacomet__

8 This person wanted his settlement to be seen by others as an example of Christian living. __John Winthrop__

9 This person was expelled from the Massachusetts Colony after being convicted of sedition. __Anne Hutchinson__

10 This person was elected governor of the Massachusetts Colony. __John Winthrop__

(continued)

CALIFORNIA STANDARDS HSS 5.3, 5.3.3, 5.4, 5.4.2; HI 2

© Harcourt

DIRECTIONS Fill in the blanks to complete the web about settling New England.

More New England Settlements

Settling Boston

Leader: **John Winthrop**

Reason for founding: **to set up an example of Christian living**

1. Became part of which colony: **Massachusetts**

Settling Providence

2. Leader: **Roger Williams**

3. Reason for founding: **expelled for "dangerous opinions"**

4. Became part of which colony: **Rhode Island**

Settling Hartford

5. Leader: **Thomas Hooker**

6. Reason for founding: **disagreed with Massachusetts Colony leaders**

7. Became part of which colony: **Connecticut**

Settling Portsmouth

8. Leader: **David Thomson**

9. Reason for founding: **sought new economic opportunities**

10. Became part of which colony: **New Hampshire**

© Harcourt

Life in New England

Name _____ Date _____

DIRECTIONS Use the Word Bank below to complete the sentences.

Word Bank
voting
praying
quilt-making
scolding
specializing

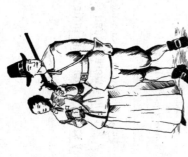

1. Puritans believed that _____ **praying** _____ was the best way to worship God.

2. Colonists _____ **specializing** _____ in various types of work were important to the community.

3. In the New England Colonies, women, indentured servants, and African slaves were not allowed to participate in _____ **voting** _____.

4. _____ **Scolding** _____ was one way that people punished those who missed church.

5. Some children enjoyed sewing and _____ **quilt-making** _____.

CALIFORNIA STANDARDS HSS 5.4, 5.4.3; CS 3

Use after reading Chapter 5, Lesson 2, pages 214–221.   Homework and Practice Book ■ **49**

(continued)

Name _____ Date _____

DIRECTIONS Read each numbered word or phrase. On the line provided, write the letter of the word or phrase that goes with it.

c   1 sawmill   a. barrels

g   2 blacksmith   b. alphabet

a   3 cooper   c. lumber

i   4 meetinghouse   d. news

e   5 constable   e. police officer

d   6 town crier   f. butter

f   7 churn   g. iron tools

j   8 animal fat   h. brushes

h   9 bristles   i. church

b   10 hornbook   j. soap

DIRECTIONS Answer the questions below.

1 What did the town crier do?
The town crier walked around the town calling out important news.

2 Why was the town crier important?
The town crier was a source of news that everyone could hear.

3 Why is the town crier no longer needed today?
Students' answers should mention that there are many different sources for news today, such as newspapers, television, and the Internet.

50 ■ Homework and Practice Book   Use after reading Chapter 5, Lesson 2, pages 214–221.

Name _____ Date _____

New England's Economy

DIRECTIONS Use the map to help you answer the questions below.

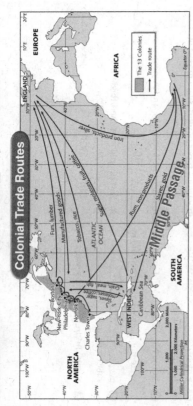

Colonial Trade Routes

1. What products did colonists export to Africa? **rum, iron products**

2. Besides slaves, what was brought from the West Indies to the colonies?
sugar, molasses, coffee

3. What goods did the New England Colonies export to England?
furs, lumber

4. After English ships unloaded iron products and silver in Africa, what was loaded
onto the ships, and where did they go next? **They were loaded
with slaves and gold, and they sailed to the West Indies.**

5. Label the route on the map that includes the Middle Passage.

CALIFORNIA STANDARDS HSS 5.4, 5.4.6; CS 4

Use after reading Chapter 5, Lesson 3, pages 222–227.   Homework and Practice Book ■ 51

© Harcourt

Name _____ Date _____

Skills: Read a Line Graph

DIRECTIONS Use the line graph to determine whether each statement is true
or false. Write *T* on the line if the statement is true. Write *F* if the statement
is false.

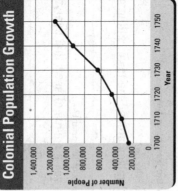

Colonial Population Growth

Source: *Historical Statistics of the United States.*
U.S. Dept. of Commerce, 1975.

F **1** There were more than 2 million people in the colonies by 1750.

T **2** Between 1700 and 1710, the population grew by fewer than 500,000 people.

T **3** There were more than twice as many people in 1740 as there were in 1720.

T **4** The population was almost a million people in 1740.

F **5** The population decreased between 1710 and 1720.

CALIFORNIA STANDARDS HSS 5.4; CS 1

52 ■ Homework and Practice Book   Use after reading Chapter 5, Skill Lesson, pages 230–231.

(continued)

© Harcourt

Name _____ Date _____

Chapter 5 — Study Guide

DIRECTIONS Fill in the missing information in these paragraphs about the New England colonies. Use the terms below to help you complete the paragraph for each lesson.

Lesson 1	Lesson 2	Lesson 3
charter	barter	exports
consent	common	imports
dissent	Harvard College	industries
expel	public offices	free-market
sedition	town meetings	naval stores

Lesson 1 The king of England gave the Puritans a __charter__ to start the Massachusetts Colony. The Puritan leaders were strict rulers who did not tolerate any __dissent__, or disagreement. When Anne Hutchinson questioned their teachings, the leaders charged her with __sedition__. It was common for the leaders to __expel__ people who disagreed with them. Roger Williams was one of those who were forced to leave. He started a new settlement with a government based on the __consent__ of the settlers.

CALIFORNIA STANDARDS HSS 5.4, 5.4.2, 5.4.3, 5.4.5

Use after reading Chapter 5, pages 206–231.

(continued)

Name _____ Date _____

DIRECTIONS Use the line graph on page 52 to help you answer the questions below.

6. What is the topic, or main idea, of the line graph?
   __colonial population growth from 1700 to 1750__

7. What kind of information do the numbers along the left side of the graph give?
   __the number of people__

8. What period of time separates the dates along the bottom of the graph?
   __ten years, or one decade__

9. In which period of time did population grow the most? How do you know?
   __from 1730 to 1740; the line rises most steeply__

10. Write one sentence that summarizes what the graph shows.
    __Possible response: The colonial population grew steadily from 1700 to 1750.__

Use after reading Chapter 5, Skill Lesson, pages 230–231.

READING SOCIAL STUDIES: SUMMARIZE

Religion in New England

DIRECTIONS Complete this graphic organizer to show that you can summarize the role of religion in the New England Colonies.

Key Fact

Possible response: The Puritans thought about the Bible's laws before taking any action.

Key Fact

Possible response: On Sundays, every person in a Puritan town had to attend church services.

Key Fact

Possible response: The Puritans harshly punished people who missed church or who spoke out in dissent.

Summary

Religion shaped life in the New England Colonies.

CALIFORNIA STANDARDS HSS 5.4, 5.4.3

56 ■ Homework and Practice Book

Use after reading Chapter 5, pages 206–231.

Lesson 2 The Puritans lived and worked together in small towns. At **town meetings**, they took care of all government business. Every year, they elected people to **public offices**. To meet their economic needs, the Puritans would **barter** with each other for goods and services. They all shared the **common**, which was used for grazing cattle and sheep. They also shared in the belief that schools were important. In 1636, the Puritans founded **Harvard College** to train ministers.

Lesson 3 New England colonists developed a **free-market** economy in which people could compete in business and set their own prices. The region's **industries** included logging and fishing. Some logs were used to produce the **naval stores** needed to build and repair ships. Trade was also an important part of the economy. **Exports** included grain, furs, whale oil, and other products. Most **imports**, or goods brought into the colonies, were English-made.

Use after reading Chapter 5, pages 206–231.

Homework and Practice Book ■ 55

© Harcourt

Name _____ Date _____

Settling the Middle Colonies

DIRECTIONS Read each description. Write its number on the map in the colony it describes. Also, fill in the blanks below each description with the name of the correct colony.

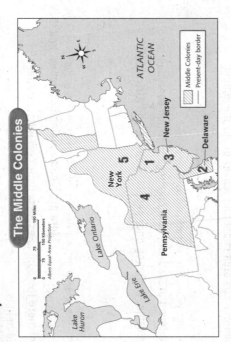

1 The first Quaker settlement in North America was founded here.
New Jersey

2 Settlers of this colony asked William Penn for their own assembly.
Delaware

3 James, Duke of York, gave this land to John Berkeley and George Carteret.
New Jersey

4 William Penn's frame of government gave its citizens important rights.
Pennsylvania

5 Before its name was changed, it was the Dutch colony of New Netherland.
New York

CALIFORNIA STANDARDS HSS 5.4, 5.4.1   Use after reading Chapter 6, Lesson 1, pages 240–246.

Homework and Practice Book ■ 57

Name _____ Date _____

Life in the Middle Colonies

DIRECTIONS Read each sentence. If the sentence is true, write *T* on the line provided. If the sentence is false, write *F*.

F 1 Philadelphia grew slowly because it was far from the nearest port.

T 2 The Middle Colonies were home to people of many different religions.

F 3 Dances and concerts were not popular in the Middle Colonies because most people believed that they were a waste of time.

T 4 Benjamin Franklin lived in Philadelphia and worked to improve the city.

T 5 Most immigrants to the Middle Colonies wanted the chance to buy their own land.

T 6 William Penn designed Philadelphia with wide streets and many public parks.

(continued)

58 ■ Homework and Practice Book   Use after reading Chapter 6, Lesson 2, pages 250–255.

CALIFORNIA STANDARDS HSS 5.4, 5.4.1, 5.4.4

Left worksheet

Name _____ Date _____

DIRECTIONS Imagine that you are George Whitefield and that you are being interviewed by a newspaper reporter. Answer the questions.

1 What is the Great Awakening?

It is a movement that calls for a

rebirth of religious life.

2 How do your sermons differ from those of more traditional ministers?

I tell people about having a direct

relationship with God.

3 You are recognized as one of the leaders of the movement. Who else is considered a leader in spreading these ideas?

Jonathan Edwards is another leader of our movement.

4 Why has your movement affected so many people?

We travel around and hold meetings at which everyone is

welcome, including poor people, women, and Africans.

5 Even though your movement is not popular with all people, how has it affected religion in the colonies? **More people have joined churches, and they**

feel more freedom to express their own religious ideas

and beliefs.

Use after reading Chapter 6, Lesson 2, pages 250–255.   Homework and Practice Book ■ 59

© Harcourt

Right worksheet

Name _____ Date _____

Busy Farms and Seaports

DIRECTIONS Read each question, and choose the best answer. Then fill in the circle for the answer that you have chosen.

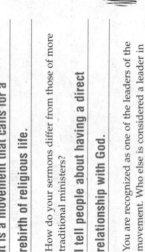

1 What was the name for a young person who was learning a skill?

- Ⓐ an apprentice
- Ⓑ an artisan
- Ⓒ a mason
- Ⓓ a tanner

2 Which of the following did the Middle Colonies import from England?

- Ⓐ grain
- Ⓑ gunpowder
- Ⓒ lumber
- Ⓓ slaves

3 What happened at a gristmill?

- Ⓐ Logs were made into lumber.
- Ⓑ Iron was made into horseshoes.
- Ⓒ Thread was made into cloth.
- Ⓓ Grain was made into flour.

4 Which of the following was NOT important to the prosperity of the Middle Colonies?

- Ⓐ farms
- Ⓑ trade
- Ⓒ whales
- Ⓓ ports

5 Which of these workers made finished goods from farm products?

- Ⓐ blacksmiths
- Ⓑ coopers
- Ⓒ masons
- Ⓓ bakers

CALIFORNIA STANDARDS HSS 5.4

60 ■ Homework and Practice Book   Use after reading Chapter 6, Lesson 3, pages 256–261.

(continued)

© Harcourt

Name _____ Date _____

Skills: Make an Economic Choice

DIRECTIONS Making wise economic choices was an important skill for people living in the Middle Colonies. Most people could not buy everything they wanted at one time. They had to make trade-offs and understand the opportunity costs of their choices. Imagine that you are a farmer in the Middle Colonies. Complete the diagram.

You have grown enough grain to trade for one of the following:

A plow
that will save time in
planting crops

A new,
warmer winter coat

If I buy the plow, the trade-off is _a new coat._

The opportunity cost is that _I will have to give up the opportunity to be really warm outdoors._

If I buy the coat, the trade-off is _a plow._

The opportunity cost is that _I will give up the opportunity to work less._

My choice is _Students may choose to buy the plow or the coat._

Why did you make this choice? _Students should say why they thought that one choice was better for them._

CALIFORNIA STANDARDS HSS 5.4; HI 4

62 ■ Homework and Practice Book

Use after reading Chapter 6, Skill Lesson, pages 262–263.

© Harcourt

Name _____ Date _____

DIRECTIONS Choose the phrase from the box that best completes each sentence.

deep harbor	Delaware River	fur traders
market towns	skilled trades	artisan households

1 _Fur traders_ who lived inland floated their goods down rivers to port cities.

2 New York City had a _deep harbor_ along the East River that offered a good place for ships to dock.

3 Farmers in the Middle Colonies usually traveled to _market towns_ to sell or trade their livestock and crops.

4 Philadelphia grew because of its location on the _Delaware River_ .

5 Some colonists made their living in _skilled trades_ , such as carpentry and shipbuilding.

6 Women and girls had fewer opportunities to work outside the home. However, they often made woven goods or candles that were sold by _artisan households_ .

Use after reading Chapter 6, Lesson 3, pages 256–261.

Homework and Practice Book ■ 61

© Harcourt

Study Guide — Chapter 6

Name _____ Date _____

DIRECTIONS Fill in the missing information in these paragraphs about the Middle Colonies. Use the terms below to help you complete the paragraph for each lesson.

Lesson 1
Tamanend
refuge
James, Duke of York
proprietor
Peter Stuyvesant

Lesson 2
militia
Great Awakening
immigrants
Benjamin Franklin
George Whitefield

Lesson 3
apprentices
tanners
masons
artisans
prosperity

Lesson 1 The Middle Colonies had a diverse population. The Dutch colony of New Netherland was led by **Peter Stuyvesant** . It welcomed settlers from many countries. In 1664, **James, Duke of York** , sent English warships to seize New Netherland. It became two English colonies, New York and New Jersey. Quakers found a **refuge** in New Jersey. William Penn was the **proprietor** of Pennsylvania. He met with **Tamanend** and established peace with neighboring Indians.

(continued)

CALIFORNIA STANDARDS HSS 5.4, 5.4.2, 5.4.3, 5.4.4

Use after reading Chapter 6, pages 240–263.

© Harcourt

Name _____ Date _____

Lesson 2 Philadelphia was the cultural center of the Middle Colonies. Many **immigrants** arrived there to start new lives. The city was home to many famous people. **Benjamin Franklin** helped start a fire department, a hospital, a library, and a college. He also organized a **militia** to protect the colony. In the 1720s, the **Great Awakening** brought a return to religious ways of life. **George Whitefield** and other ministers spread their ideas throughout the Middle Colonies.

Lesson 3 The economy of the Middle Colonies was as diverse as the region's people. Farming and trade were the main reasons for the region's **prosperity** . But this economic success also created many other kinds of jobs. **Artisans** used raw materials to make products from iron tools to barrels. **Masons** used stone to construct roads, walls, and buildings. **Tanners** turned animal skins into leather for shoes and other products. Young people learned these skills by becoming **apprentices** .

Use after reading Chapter 6, pages 240–263.

© Harcourt

Settling the South

DIRECTIONS Choose words and phrases from the box to complete the chart.

as a refuge for Catholics	African slaves
wealthy English family	divided into two colonies
the Lords Proprietors	to get land for farming
James Oglethorpe	1633
to give debtors a new start	English

Settling the South

Where	Who	Why	When
	1. Founder: the Calverts, a **wealthy English family**	2. **as a refuge for Catholics**	3.
Maryland	First proprietor: Cecilius Calvert First governor: Leonard Calvert	and to make money	**1633**
Carolina	4. Founders: **the Lords Proprietors** 5. First colonists: English settlers, landowners from the West Indies, and **African slaves**	6. **to get land for farming**	7. founded 1663; **divided into two colonies,** 1712
Georgia	8. Founder: **James Oglethorpe** 9. First colonists: **English**	10. **to give debtors a new start**	1733

(continued)

CALIFORNIA STANDARDS HSS 5.4, 5.4.1, 5.4.2, 5.4.3; HI 2   Use after reading Chapter 7, Lesson 1, pages 272–279.

READING SOCIAL STUDIES: SUMMARIZE

The Middle Colonies

DIRECTIONS Complete this graphic organizer to show that you can summarize facts about the Middle Colonies.

Key Fact
The Middle Colonies had long summers.

Key Fact
The Middle Colonies had plenty of rain.

Key Fact
The Middle Colonies had rich farmland.

Summary
The Middle Colonies were a good place for growing crops.

Key Fact
Religious toleration increased in the Middle Colonies.

Key Fact
The diversity of religious beliefs became greater.

Key Fact
The free exercise of religion grew.

Summary
The Great Awakening changed the religious life of the colonies.

CALIFORNIA STANDARDS HSS 5.4, 5.4.1
Use after reading Chapter 6, pages 240–263.

© Harcourt

Homework and Practice Book Teacher Edition ■ 33

Name _____ Date _____

DIRECTIONS Use the completed chart on page 66 to help you answer these questions.

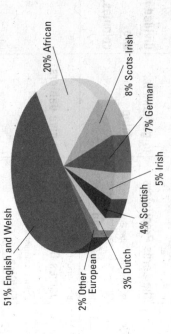
James Oglethorpe

1. Which colony was set up to help debtors?
Georgia

2. What happened in Carolina in 1712?
It was divided into two colonies.

3. What colony did the Calverts found?
Maryland

4. What group sought religious freedom in Maryland?
Catholics

5. Who were the Lords Proprietors?
the leaders who founded the colony of Carolina

6. Which colony was founded 100 years after the Maryland Colony?
Georgia

7. Who were the Calverts?
They were a wealthy English family.

8. Where did many colonists settle in order to get land for farming?
Carolina

9. Who founded the Georgia Colony? When was it founded?
James Oglethorpe; 1733

10. In which colony were Africans among the first colonists?
Carolina

Use after reading Chapter 7, Lesson 1, pages 272–279.   Homework and Practice Book ■ 67

© Harcourt

Name _____ Date _____

Skills: Read Circle Graphs

DIRECTIONS Use the circle graph to help you answer the questions.

Population of the 13 Colonies by Ethnicity, 1750

- 20% African
- 8% Scots-Irish
- 7% German
- 5% Irish
- 4% Scottish
- 3% Dutch
- 2% Other European
- 51% English and Welsh

1. What was the largest ethnic group in the 13 colonies in 1750?
English and Welsh

2. What was the smallest group?
Other European

3. What percent of the total colonial population was Dutch?
3%

4. What percent of the total colonial population was African?
20%

5. What was the combined percent of all people who were not English or Welsh?
49%

(continued)

CALIFORNIA STANDARDS HSS 5.4, 5.4.2, 5.4.3; HI 2

68 ■ Homework and Practice Book   Use after reading Chapter 7, Skill Lesson, pages 280–281.

© Harcourt

Name _____ Date _____

Pennsylvania Churches in 1750*

Church	Percent of Population
A. Dutch Reformed	32%
B. Lutheran	28%
C. Baptist	15%
D. Anglican	10%
E. German Reformed	6%
F. Catholic	6%
G. Congregationalist	3%

*Quaker meetinghouses not included

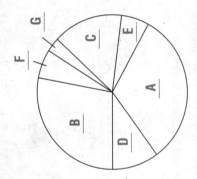

DIRECTIONS Use the information in the circle graph to answer these questions.

1. What kind of church had the largest number of members? __Dutch Reformed__

2. What percent of Pennsylvania colonists were Catholic? __6%__

3. What other church had about the same number of members as the Catholic Church? __German Reformed__

4. What two church groups made up twenty-five percent of Pennsylvania's population? __Baptist and Anglican__

Name _____ Date _____

Life in the South

DIRECTIONS Read the passage below. Use the information it contains to complete the Venn diagram, comparing and contrasting life in the South.

Plantations and Small Farms

Most Southern colonists lived and worked on small farms. They planted and harvested their own crops. The owners of small farms did most of the work themselves, because few of them owned slaves. Many families on small farms lived in one-story houses, far from their neighbors.

People on plantations often lived far from others, too. However, there were often many families living on plantation land. Sometimes plantations looked like small villages, with many buildings surrounding the owner's home. Some were workshops, where slaves made nails, bricks, barrels, and other items used on the plantation. The kitchen was in a building by itself. Plantation owners often lived in large houses. Many of the plantations in the Southern Colonies were self-sufficient. Planters grew food, and skilled workers produced needed goods. Slaves did most of the work on the plantations.

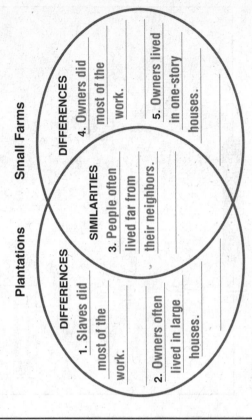

Plantations   Small Farms

DIFFERENCES
1. Slaves did most of the work.

2. Owners often lived in large houses.

SIMILARITIES
3. People often lived far from their neighbors.

DIFFERENCES
4. Owners did most of the work.

5. Owners lived in one-story houses.

CALIFORNIA STANDARDS HSS 5.4

70 ▪ Homework and Practice Book   Use after reading Chapter 7, Lesson 2, pages 282–288.

The Southern Economy

Name _____ Date _____

DIRECTIONS Answer the questions below.

1. What role did brokers play in the Southern economy? **Brokers were paid to sell planters' crops in England and to send back English goods that the planters wanted.**

2. What cash crop grew well on warm, wet land? **rice**

3. Why did the introduction of indigo as a cash crop help the Southern economy? **Indigo grew well on land where rice did not.**

4. Besides agriculture and trade, what were two industries in the Southern Colonies? **Possible responses: fur trapping and hunting, forest products, naval stores, shipbuilding**

5. How did slaves contribute to the economic success of the Southern Colonies? **They did most of the work on plantations, and plantations grew the crops that brought cash into the Southern Colonies.**

CALIFORNIA STANDARDS HSS 5.4, 5.4.1, 5.4.5, 5.4.6; HI 2

Use after reading Chapter 7, Lesson 3, pages 290–295.

Homework and Practice Book ■ 71

Skills: Read a Land Use and Products Map

Name _____ Date _____

DIRECTIONS Use the map on this page to help you answer the questions on page 73.

Colonial Products

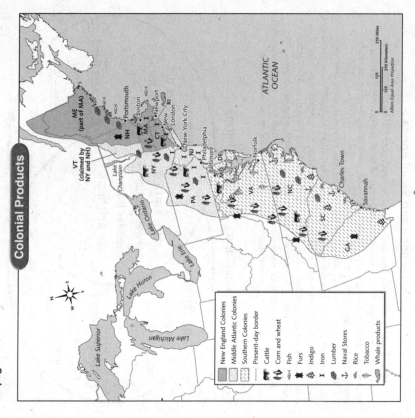

Legend:
- New England Colonies
- Middle Atlantic Colonies
- Southern Colonies
- Present-day border
- Cattle
- Corn and wheat
- Fish
- Furs
- Indigo
- Iron
- Lumber
- Naval Stores
- Rice
- Tobacco
- Whale products

CALIFORNIA STANDARDS HSS 5.4; CS 4

Use after reading Chapter 7, Skill Lesson, pages 296–297.

72 ■ Homework and Practice Book

(continued)

© Harcourt

1. Which colonies produced indigo?
North Carolina, South Carolina, and Georgia

2. Where was rice grown? **North Carolina and South Carolina**

3. Which colonies manufactured iron? **New Jersey, Pennsylvania, New York, Connecticut, Rhode Island, Massachusetts**

4. Which colonies raised cattle? **Massachusetts, New York, Connecticut, Pennsylvania, Maryland, and North Carolina**

5. In which colonies were you likely to find whale products?
Rhode Island and Massachusetts

6. Which colonies grew the cash crop tobacco?
Maryland, Virginia, and North Carolina

7. Which colonies produced naval stores? **Massachusetts, North Carolina, and South Carolina**

8. What part of the Massachusetts Colony produced a great deal of lumber and fish?
Maine

9. What crops were grown along almost the entire length of the colonies?
corn and wheat

10. Which colonies had a great variety of products?
Possible response: North Carolina, South Carolina, Massachusetts, Pennsylvania

---

Chapter 7

Study Guide

DIRECTIONS Fill in the missing information in these paragraphs about the Southern Colonies. Use the terms below to help you complete the paragraph for each lesson.

Lesson 1	Lesson 2	Lesson 3
Maryland	Black Seminoles	shipbuilding
James Oglethorpe	overseers	Charles Town
backcountry	Fort Mose	indigo
constitution	planters	tobacco
Toleration Act	institutionalized	Wilmington

Lesson 1 The Calvert family founded the ____**Maryland**____ Colony along Chesapeake Bay. The colony's assembly passed the ____**Toleration Act**____, which granted religious freedom to all Christians. The Lords Proprietors founded Carolina and wrote a ____**constitution**____, or plan of government, for it. ____**James Oglethorpe**____ founded Georgia to provide a new home for English debtors. In the mid-1700s, settlers began to move inland to a region they called the ____**backcountry**____.

CALIFORNIA STANDARDS HSS 5.4, 5.4.1, 5.4.2, 5.4.5, 5.4.6   Use after reading Chapter 7, pages 272–297.

(continued)

© Harcourt

Homework and Practice Book Teacher Edition ■ 37

READING SOCIAL STUDIES: SUMMARIZE

Focus Skill

Life in the Southern Colonies

DIRECTIONS Complete this graphic organizer to show that you can summarize facts about the Southern Colonies.

Summary
Planters were an important part of the economy in the South.

Key Fact
Planters grew cash crops such as tobacco.

Key Fact
Planters traded cash crops for goods and services.

Key Fact
Planters sold their cash crops in England.

Summary
Enslaved Africans dealt with the hardships of their lives in many ways.

Key Fact
Slaves often resisted slavery by working slowly or running away.

Key Fact
They preserved their culture by telling stories about Africa and singing African songs.

Key Fact
Many turned to the Christian religion for strength.

CALIFORNIA STANDARDS HSS 5.4

Use after reading Chapter 7, pages 272–297.

Lesson 2 Most Southern colonists lived either on plantations or on small farms. **Planters** were the wealthiest people in society. They hired **overseers** to watch slaves at work in their fields. In time, slavery became **institutionalized**, or a part of life, in the colonies. Some slaves escaped from plantations or bought their freedom. Those who went to live among the Indians were called **Black Seminoles**. Others started the settlement of **Fort Mose** in Spanish Florida.

Lesson 3 Cash crops were important to the Southern economy. **Tobacco** grew in Maryland, Virginia, and northern North Carolina. Rice and **indigo** grew farther south. **Charles Town** became an important port city for shipping rice. Grain and tobacco were shipped from Baltimore, and **shipbuilding** was also an important industry in that city. **Wilmington** was an important shipping center for forest products.

Use after reading Chapter 7, pages 272–297.

© Harcourt

Name _____ Date _____

Competition for Control

DIRECTIONS Number the sentences in the order in which the events occurred.

Chief Pontiac

1 — 6   To make up for Spain's losses in the war, France gave Spain most of its lands west of the Mississippi River.

2 — 5   The British captured several forts, including Fort Duquesne.

3 — 7   The French and Indian War ended with the Treaty of Paris, giving Britain most of present-day Canada and all French lands east of the Mississippi River and Spanish Florida.

4 — 9   King George III issued the Proclamation of 1763, which said that all land west of the Appalachian Mountains belonged to the Indians.

5 — 2   The French built Fort Duquesne at the present-day site of Pittsburgh, Pennsylvania.

6 — 3   The French and Indian War began with the battle of Fort Necessity.

7 — 1   The French sent soldiers to drive British traders out of the Ohio Valley.

8 — 10   The British Parliament passed the Sugar Act, which was designed to make colonists help pay for Britain's defense of the colonies.

9 — 8   Chief Pontiac joined with other American Indian tribes and attacked British forts.

10 — 4   Colonial leaders rejected Benjamin Franklin's Albany Plan of Union.

CALIFORNIA STANDARDS HSS 5.3, 5.3.1, 5.3.3; CS 1

Use after reading Chapter 8, Lesson 1, pages 318–323.   Homework and Practice Book ■ 77

Name _____ Date _____

Skills: Compare Historical Maps

DIRECTIONS Use the maps below to help you answer the questions that follow.

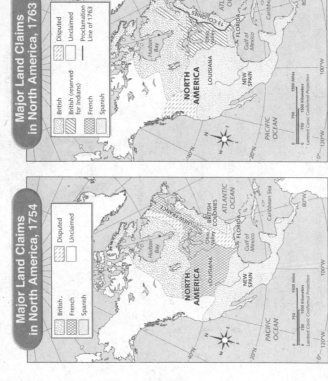

Major Land Claims in North America, 1754

Legend:
- British
- French
- Spanish
- Disputed
- Unclaimed

Major Land Claims in North America, 1763

Legend:
- British
- British (reserved for Indians)
- French
- Spanish
- Disputed
- Unclaimed
- Proclamation Line of 1763

1 Which country claimed Louisiana in 1754?

France

2 Which countries gained land between 1754 and 1763?

Spain and Britain

CALIFORNIA STANDARDS HSS 5.3, 5.3.1, 5.3.3; CS 4; HI 3

78 ■ Homework and Practice Book   Use after reading Chapter 8, Skill Lesson, pages 324–325.

(continued)

Colonists Speak Out

DIRECTIONS Read each numbered description. On the line provided, write the letter of the person, group, or law that goes with it.

1. **e** a tax on colonial newspapers
2. **d** killed at Boston Massacre
3. **g** captured British tax collectors
4. **j** a tax on imports to the colonies
5. **a** was accused of treason
6. **h** pushed Parliament to tax colonies
7. **b** "No taxation without representation."
8. **f** protested tax laws in Parliament
9. **c** told colonists not to drink tea
10. **i** made a picture of the Boston Massacre

a. Patrick Henry
b. James Otis
c. Daughters of Liberty
d. Crispus Attucks
e. Stamp Act
f. Benjamin Franklin
g. Sons of Liberty
h. George Grenville
i. Paul Revere
j. Townshend Acts

Benjamin Franklin

CALIFORNIA STANDARDS HSS 5.5, 5.5.1, 5.5.4

Use after reading Chapter 8, Lesson 2, pages 326–332.

---

3. Which country lost all its lands in North America between 1754 and 1763?

   France

4. What event explains the differences between Map A and Map B?

   the French and Indian War

5. What regions did Britain claim both in 1754 and in 1763?

   land bordering the Atlantic Ocean and the land north of Louisiana and around Hudson Bay

6. What happened to Louisiana between 1754 and 1763?

   It changed from French control to Spanish control.

7. What two countries claimed land that bordered the disputed area of the Pacific Northwest in 1763?

   Spain and England

8. For what group was the land in the Ohio Valley area reserved by King George III?

   American Indians

9. What area changed from Spanish control to British control?

   Florida

10. Did any areas change from British control to Spanish control?

    no

Use after reading Chapter 8, Skill Lesson, pages 324–325.

© Harcourt

Name _____ Date _____

Skills: Distinguish Fact from Fiction

DIRECTIONS Read the passages below about General Washington's crossing of the Delaware River. Then answer the questions.

Passage A "As the four boys sat huddled together, the oarsmen dressed in tattered blue and buff uniforms used their long poles to push off the ice. Matt recognized them from the history report he and Q had worked on together.

"'They must be John Glover's Marbleheaders!' he whispered to Q.

"'This must be the Delaware River,' Q whispered back. Both boys remembered reading about the special group of seafaring enlisted men from the north, under the guidance of Colonel John Glover of Marblehead, Massachusetts. They had manned the sturdy Durham boats that had carried Washington and his troops across the river on that Christmas night.'"*

*Elvira Woodruff. *George Washington's Socks.* Scholastic, 1991.

Passage B "I am sitting in the ferry house. The troops are all over, and boats have gone back for the artillery. We are three hours behind the set time . . . [the Marblehead fishermen] directing the boats have had a hard time to force boats through the floating ice with the snow drifting in their faces . . ."*

*excerpt from *The Diary of Colonel John Fitzgerald* in *The American Revolution in the Delaware Valley* by Edward S. Gifford, Jr. Pennsylvania Society of Sons of the Revolution, 1976.

1. Which passage is from a documentary source?

   Passage B

2. Which passage is from a fictional source?

   Passage A

3. What is one clue that helped you make your decision?

   Possible response: The boys in Passage A recognized the fishermen from a history report they had worked on, which suggests they are students who have traveled back in time.

CALIFORNIA STANDARDS HSS 5.5, 5.5.4; HR 3

Use after reading Chapter 8, Skill Lesson, pages 334–335.

Homework and Practice Book ▪ 81

Name _____ Date _____

Disagreements Grow

DIRECTIONS Answer the following questions about the First Continental Congress.

1. How did the First Continental Congress get its name?

   It was the first formal meeting of colonial representatives on the North American continent.

2. Why did the First Continental Congress meet?

   to talk about how to respond to the Coercive Acts

3. Where did the First Continental Congress meet?

   in Philadelphia

4. In its signed petition to the king, what rights did the First Continental Congress claim colonists had?

   the right to life and liberty, the right to assemble, and the right to a jury trial

5. The First Continental Congress asked the British Parliament to respond to its petition by what date?

   May 10, 1775

6. How did the First Continental Congress make war with Britain more likely?

   It asked the colonies to form militias, which provided the colonies with soldiers who could fight the British. Also, Congress stopped most trade with Britain.

CALIFORNIA STANDARDS HSS 5.5, 5.5.2; HI 1

Use after reading Chapter 8, Lesson 3, pages 336–341.

82 ▪ Homework and Practice Book

The Road to War

Name _____ Date _____

DIRECTIONS Choose the phrase from the box that best completes each sentence. Write the phrase in the blank.

Olive Branch Petition	Continental currency
Continental Army	Bunker Hill
Second Continental Congress	

1 The ___Second Continental Congress___ met as a result of the fighting at Lexington and Concord.

2 The ___Continental Army___ differed from militias in that it was made up of full-time soldiers.

3 The ___Olive Branch Petition___ asked Britain's King George III for peace on behalf of the colonists.

4 As part of its preparations for war, Congress printed ___Continental currency___.

5 After the battle at ___Bunker Hill___, the king sent a proclamation promising to crush the rebellion in the colonies.

CALIFORNIA STANDARDS HSS 5.5, 5.5.1

Use after reading Chapter 8, Lesson 4, pages 342–346. Homework and Practice Book ▪ 83

© Harcourt

Declaring Independence

Name _____ Date _____

DIRECTIONS Read each sentence below. On the line provided, write the name of the person whom the sentence tells about.

| John Adams | John Dickinson | John Hancock |
| Thomas Paine | Thomas Jefferson | Richard Henry Lee |

1 "I told the Second Continental Congress that the 13 colonies no longer owed any loyalty to the British king."
___Richard Henry Lee___

2 "I was the president of the Second Continental Congress and the first person to sign the Declaration of Independence."
___John Hancock___

3 "I was the main writer of the Declaration of Independence."
___Thomas Jefferson___

4 "I thought that Americans should always celebrate Independence Day."
___John Adams___

5 "I wrote *Common Sense*, which said that people should rule themselves."
___Thomas Paine___

6 "I headed the committee that wrote the Articles of Confederation."
___John Dickinson___

CALIFORNIA STANDARDS HSS 5.5, 5.5.3, 5.5.4

84 ▪ Homework and Practice Book   Use after reading Chapter 8, Lesson 5, pages 348–353.

© Harcourt

Name _____

Date _____

Skills: Identify Multiple Causes and Their Effects

DIRECTIONS Using the chart below, answer questions about causes and effects.

The Declaration of Independence

Causes

Richard Henry Lee calls for a resolution stating that the colonies are independent.

Congress chooses a committee to draft the Declaration of Independence.

Thomas Jefferson writes most of the Declaration of Independence.

→

Effects

Congress approves the Declaration of Independence.

The Declaration of Independence is read publicly for the first time.

→

Crowds celebrate the colonies' independence.

1 Which effect do you think first followed the causes? Why?
The writing of the Declaration of Independence. It had to be written before it could be approved or read.

2 In your opinion, which effect had the greatest impact on the people?
Possible response: The public reading of the Declaration of Independence, because it gave the people joy.

CALIFORNIA STANDARDS HSS 5.5, 5.5.1; HI 3

Use after reading Chapter 8, Skill Lesson, pages 354–355.

Name _____

Date _____

Study Guide

DIRECTIONS Fill in the missing information in these paragraphs. Use the terms below to help you complete the paragraphs.

Lesson 1	Lesson 2	Lesson 3	Lesson 4	Lesson 5
proclamation	treason	monopoly	olive branch	grievances
alliances	budget	blockade	commander	independence
delegates	boycott	petition	in chief	resolution
	representation		earthworks	

Lesson 1 In the French and Indian War, Britain and France fought over land claims in North America. Both sides made **alliances** with American Indians. At a meeting in Albany, New York, Benjamin Franklin urged the British colonies to unite against the French. But the other **delegates** rejected his plan. After Britain won the war, its king issued a **proclamation** setting aside certain lands for Indians.

Lesson 2 The French and Indian War was costly for Britain. After the war, Parliament reviewed its **budget** . It decided to tax colonists to raise more money. Many colonists said that Parliament could not tax them because the colonists had no **representation** , or voice, in Parliament. When Patrick Henry argued that colonists should not pay, some people accused him of **treason** . Many others agreed with Henry, though. More and more colonists began to **boycott** British goods to protest new taxes.

CALIFORNIA STANDARDS HSS 5.3, 5.3.3, 5.5, 5.5.1, 5.5.2, 5.5.3, 5.5.4   Use after reading Chapter 8, pages 318–357.

(continued)

READING SOCIAL STUDIES: CAUSE AND EFFECT
✪ Uniting the Colonies
Focus Skill

DIRECTIONS Complete this graphic organizer to show that you understand some of the causes and effects of the American Revolution.

Cause		Effect
Britain needed money to pay for the French and Indian War.	→	Parliament passed the Sugar Act.
Parliament passed the Tea Act.	→	Colonists staged the Boston Tea Party.
Britain passed the Intolerable Acts.	→	The colonies sent representatives to the First Continental Congress.
British soldiers and colonists often clashed in Boston.	→	The Boston Massacre took place.

CALIFORNIA STANDARDS HSS 5.5, 5.5.1

Use after reading Chapter 8, pages 318–357.

© Harcourt

Lesson 3 The Tea Act gave Britain a ____**monopoly**____ on tea in the colonies. In response, the Sons of Liberty threw boxes of British tea into Boston Harbor. British leaders were so angry that they ordered the navy to ____**blockade**____ the harbor. Colonial leaders met at the First Continental Congress and decided to send a ____**petition**____ to the king, stating colonists' rights.

Lesson 4 The Second Continental Congress set up the Continental Army and named George Washington its ____**commander in chief**____. The war's first major battle, at Lexington and Concord, had already taken place. At Breed's Hill, colonists fired at British soldiers from defenses called ____**earthworks**____. The British won Breed's Hill, but more than 1,000 British soldiers died. Afterwards, Congress asked King George III for peace. Its petition was named after the ____**olive branch**____, an ancient symbol of peace.

Lesson 5 As conflicts between Britain and the colonies grew, more and more colonists wanted ____**independence**____ from Britain. In Congress, Richard Henry Lee called for a ____**resolution**____ to free the united colonies. Congress chose a committee to write to King George III about the matter. This statement became known as the Declaration of Independence. It listed many ____**grievances**____, or complaints, that the colonists had against the king and Parliament.

Use after reading Chapter 8, pages 318–357.

© Harcourt

Name _____ Date _____

Skills: Read Parallel Time Lines

DIRECTIONS Use the time lines to answer the questions.

America and the Revolution

1770	1775	1780	1785

1774
The First Continental Congress meets

1775
The Battles of Lexington and Concord are fought

1776
The Declaration of Independence is signed

1778
The colonies sign a treaty with France

1781
Americans force British to surrender at Yorktown, the last major battle of the war

1. Who was the king of France during the Revolutionary War?

   Louis XVI

2. When did the Marquis de Lafayette arrive in the colonies?

   1777

3. Which event appears on both time lines?

   the signing of a treaty between France and the colonies

4. Did the first French troops arrive in the colonies before or after the Declaration of Independence was signed? **after**

5. Which time line shows the earliest battles in the war?

   America and the Revolution

CALIFORNIA STANDARDS HSS 5.6, 5.6.2; CS 1   Use after reading Chapter 9, Skill Lesson, pages 374–375.

(continued)

Name _____ Date _____

Americans and the Revolution

DIRECTIONS Read each statement below. On the line provided, write *P* if the statement is something that a Patriot would have said. Write *L* if the statement is something that a Loyalist would have said, and write *N* if it is something that a neutral person would have said.

1. **P** "I never thought I would burn my own crops, but it's better than providing food for redcoats."

2. **N** "I don't care who wins; I just want this war to end."

3. **L** "The soldiers have a right to take what they need from people who are nothing but rebels."

4. **L** "I do not understand why my son has chosen to fight on the side of people who betray their king."

5. **P** "People who profiteer are traitors to the cause of freedom."

CALIFORNIA STANDARDS HSS 5.6, 5.6.4

© Harcourt

Homework and Practice Book Teacher Edition ▪ 45

Fighting for Independence

DIRECTIONS Place each name from the box where it belongs on the chart.

John Burgoyne
Friedrich Wilhelm von Steuben
George Washington
Benedict Arnold
Jorge Farragut

Bernardo de Gálvez
William Howe
Marquis de Lafayette
George Clinton
Benjamin Franklin

Helped the Americans	Helped the British
Bernardo de Gálvez	John Burgoyne
Friedrich Wilhelm von Steuben	William Howe
George Washington	
Marquis de Lafayette	
Benedict Arnold	
George Clinton	
Jorge Farragut	
Benjamin Franklin	

CALIFORNIA STANDARDS HSS 5.6, 5.6.1

Use after reading Chapter 9, Lesson 2, pages 378–384.

(continued)

France and the Revolution

1770 | 1775 | 1780 | 1785

1774 King Louis XV dies. His grandson, Louis XVI, becomes king

1777 Marquis de Lafayette and his forces arrive to help colonists fight the British

1778 France signs a treaty with the colonies

1780 French soldiers arrive at Newport, Rhode Island

1781 French soldiers help Continental Army surround Yorktown, site of the last major battle of the war

1781 French navy keeps fresh troops and supplies from reaching the British, and it brings more troops to aid Americans at Yorktown

6. Which was signed first, the treaty with France or the Declaration of Independence?
the Declaration of Independence

7. Where did French troops arrive first, in Newport or in Yorktown?
in Newport

List three ways in which the French helped bring about the British surrender at Yorktown.

8. Possible response: The French navy kept the British from getting fresh troops and supplies.

9. Possible response: French ships brought soldiers to help the Americans.

10. Possible response: French soldiers helped Americans surround Yorktown.

Use after reading Chapter 9, Skill Lesson, pages 374–375.

Name _____ Date _____

DIRECTIONS Use phrases from the paragraph below to complete the Venn diagram. Write each phrase in the correct section of the diagram.

The soldiers in both the Continental Army and the British army carried muskets with bayonets into battle, but in other ways these armies were very different. The British army had 50,000 soldiers in the colonies. The soldiers were well trained and experienced in battle. They were also helped by thousands of mercenaries. The Continental Army was made up of less than 15,000 soldiers. Many of these soldiers were farmers who had just signed up for the army. The armies also looked different and carried different things with them. The Continental soldier often wore a tricorn hat and carried a cartridge bag with a sling. The British soldier wore a bright red coat, and carried a haversack for food.

Continental Army   **British Army**

1. 15,000 soldiers

2. many were farmers

3. wore tricorn hats

4. carried cartridge bags with slings

Both

5. used muskets with bayonets

6. 50,000 soldiers

7. well trained and experienced

8. helped by mercenaries

9. wore bright red coats

10. carried haversacks for food

Use after reading Chapter 9, Lesson 2, pages 378–384.   Homework and Practice Book ▪ 93

Name _____ Date _____

Skills: Compare Maps with Different Scales

DIRECTIONS Answer the questions below by choosing the map on page 95 that best answers the question.

1. Which map could you use to find the distance from Saratoga to Albany?
   Map A

2. Which map could you use to find the distance from Fort Ticonderoga to Saratoga? **Map A** What is the distance in miles?
   about 70 miles

3. Which map could you use to find the distance from Barber Farm to the Hudson River? **Map B** Explain why. **Map B has a smaller scale and shows more detail of the area.**

4. Which map could you use to find the distance from Barber Farm to the Great Ravine? **Map B** What is the distance in miles?
   about one mile

5. What is the distance in miles from the second battle of Saratoga to the town of Saratoga? **about 10 miles** Which map did you use?
   Map A

6. Which map would you choose if you wanted to better understand the events that took place at the second battle of Saratoga on October 7, 1777? **Map B** Why? **Map B shows the area of the second battle of Saratoga in greater detail.**

7. Which map would you choose if you were going to plan a reenactment of the battle? **Map B** Explain why. **Map B shows the movement of the British and American forces during the battle.**

(continued)

CALIFORNIA STANDARDS HSS 5.6, 5.6.1; CS 4   Use after reading Chapter 9, Skill Lesson, pages 386–387.

94 ▪ Homework and Practice Book

Winning Independence

DIRECTIONS Follow the instructions below. Complete the exercise by placing your answers on the map or by writing your answers on the line provided.

Winning Independence

1. Draw an X at the city where Nathan Hale died.
   New York City

2. Draw a pitcher at the battle where Mary Ludwig Hays McCauley took water to soldiers.
   Monmouth

3. Draw a hammer next to the place where Tadeusz Kosciuszko planned a fort.
   West Point

4. Circle the place where Nathanael Greene and Daniel Morgan led Americans to victory.
   Cowpens

5. Draw a star next to the place where General Cornwallis surrendered.
   Yorktown

6. Where was the only major battle fought in North Carolina during the Revolutionary War?
   Guilford Courthouse

CALIFORNIA STANDARDS HSS 5.6, 5.6.1, 5.6.2

Use after reading Chapter 9, Lesson 3, pages 388–395.

Map A: The Second Battle of Saratoga, 1777

Map B: The Second Battle of Saratoga, 1777

Use after reading Chapter 9, Skill Lesson, pages 386–387.

Name _____ Date _____

Consequences of the War

DIRECTIONS Read each question and choose the best answer. Then fill in the circle for the answer that you have chosen.

1 Which idea in the Declaration of Independence changed people's views of slavery?
 (A) the idea that people must obey the government
 (B) the idea that all men have a right to life and liberty
 (C) the idea that the colonies would no longer be ruled by Britain
 (D) the idea that people should not be taxed without their consent

2 What argument did Elizabeth Freeman use to win her freedom in court?
 (A) She argued that all people are born free.
 (B) She argued that her owner was cruel.
 (C) She argued that slavery had been abolished.
 (D) She argued that she had a right to vote.

3 Which state was the first to abolish slavery?
 (A) Georgia
 (B) Maryland
 (C) Massachusetts
 (D) Virginia

4 Who formed the nation's first abolitionist group?
 (A) slaves
 (B) Indians
 (C) planters
 (D) Quakers

5 What did the Northwest Ordinance say about slavery?
 (A) It allowed slavery in the Northwest Territory.
 (B) It outlawed slavery in the Northwest Territory.
 (C) It said that each state in the Northwest Territory could decide whether to allow slavery.
 (D) It did not mention slavery.

CALIFORNIA STANDARDS HSS 5.6, 5.6.6, 5.6.7

Use after reading Chapter 9, Lesson 4, pages 396–401.

Name _____ Date _____

Study Guide

DIRECTIONS Fill in the missing information in these paragraphs about the American Revolution. Use the names and terms below to help you complete the paragraphs.

Lesson 1	Lesson 2	Lesson 3	Lesson 4
Sybil Ludington	turning point	Nathan Hale	abolitionists
Thayendanegea	mercenaries	Benedict Arnold	ordinance
Peter Salem	negotiate	John Paul Jones	territories
James Armistead	campaign		
Deborah Sampson			

Lesson 1 The Revolutionary War affected nearly everyone in the colonies. Women played important roles in the war. A teenager named __Sybil Ludington__ warned American troops that the British were about to attack. __Deborah Sampson__ disguised herself as a man and fought in the war. African Americans, too, made important contributions. __James Armistead__ won his freedom by working as a spy for George Washington. __Peter Salem__ and several other African Americans fought at Concord. American Indian groups allied with both the Americans and the British. __Thayendanegea__ and the Mohawks fought on the side of the British, while the Oneida and Tuscarora fought for the Americans.

CALIFORNIA STANDARDS HSS 5.6, 5.6.1, 5.6.2, 5.6.3, 5.6.5, 5.6.6, 5.6.7   Use after reading Chapter 9, pages 366–401.

(continued)

Name _____ Date _____

READING SOCIAL STUDIES: CAUSE AND EFFECT

The Revolutionary War

DIRECTIONS Complete this graphic organizer to show that you understand the causes and effects of some of the key events of the Revolutionary War.

Cause		Effect
Congress printed more currency.	→	The money became less valuable.

Cause		Effect
News of the American victory at Saratoga reached France.	→	France agreed to help the Americans.

Cause		Effect
The Treaty of Paris was signed.	→	Borders were set for a new country known as the United States of America.

CALIFORNIA STANDARDS HSS 5.6, 5.6.4

Use after reading Chapter 9, pages 366–401.

Name _____ Date _____

Lesson 2 In 1777, the British began a ___campaign___ to capture New York. The large British Army was helped by ___mercenaries___ from Germany. Yet the British lost an important battle at Saratoga. This battle was a ___turning point___ in the war. Benjamin Franklin had gone to France to ___negotiate___ with French leaders. He wanted France to help Americans in the war. The American victory at Saratoga convinced French leaders that colonists could win the war, and they agreed to help.

Lesson 3 The American Revolution created many strong leaders, and a few traitors. ___Nathan Hale___ was a Patriot spy who was captured by the British and hanged. Navy commander ___John Paul Jones___ fought the British Navy off the coast of Britain. But ___Benedict Arnold___, who had led his troops to victory at Saratoga, betrayed his country and helped the British.

Lesson 4 State constitutions that were written after 1776 embodied the ideals of the American Revolution. The ideals stated in the Declaration of Independence led some Americans to believe that slavery was wrong. Some became ___abolitionists___ and spoke out against slavery. Efforts to end slavery affected ___territories___ outside the states. In 1787, an ___ordinance___ governing lands to the northwest outlawed slavery in the region.

Use after reading Chapter 9, pages 366–401.

Homework and Practice Book ▪ 99

The Articles of Confederation

Name _____ Date _____

DIRECTIONS Answer the questions below.

James Madison was one leader who wanted to replace the Articles of Confederation.

1. How was the plan of government outlined by the Articles of Confederation supposed to help the 13 new states?

   It was supposed to help the states work together on national issues.

2. What was the main shortcoming of the Articles of Confederation?

   The Articles of Confederation created a weak national government, which prevented the government from working efficiently.

3. What were the people who took part in Shays's Rebellion angry about?

   The government had not paid their army salaries; they had to pay high state taxes; and if they could not pay their debts, the courts took away their farms.

4. How did Shays's Rebellion call attention to problems with the national government?

   It showed that there was no national army to defend United States property from the protesters or to stop the rebellion.

5. What did 12 states decide to do after Shays's Rebellion?

   They decided to hold a convention to change the Articles of Confederation and strengthen the national government.

CALIFORNIA STANDARDS HSS 5.7, 5.7.1; HI 1

Use after reading Chapter 10, Lesson 1, pages 420–425.

Homework and Practice Book ■ 101

The Constitutional Convention

Name _____ Date _____

DIRECTIONS Write one sentence about each leader listed below. Name a contribution that the leader made to the Constitutional Convention.

1. George Washington

   Possible response: He was elected by the delegates to serve as the president of the convention.

2. Roger Sherman

   Possible response: He introduced the Connecticut Compromise, which was the basis for the Great Compromise.

3. Gouverneur Morris

   Possible response: He spoke out against slavery.

4. Edmund Randolph

   Possible response: He introduced a plan for Congress called the Virginia Plan, which favored populous states.

5. William Paterson

   Possible response: He introduced a plan for Congress called the New Jersey Plan, which favored states with few people.

CALIFORNIA STANDARDS HSS 5.7

102 ■ Homework and Practice Book

Use after reading Chapter 10, Lesson 2, pages 426–433.

Three Branches of Government

DIRECTIONS Use the words and phrases in the box to complete the diagram.

Supreme Court   President   Senate   Executive Branch

Legislative Branch
- Senate
- House of Representatives

Executive Branch
- President
- Vice President

Judicial Branch
- Supreme Court
- District Courts

DIRECTIONS Read the list below of positions in the government. In the space provided, write a brief description of the duties of the person holding that job.

1 President

The President has veto power, is commander in chief of the

United States military, and carries out the nation's laws faithfully.

2 Supreme Court justice

Justices decide cases dealing with the Constitution, national

law, or treaties. They also decide cases between states and

between citizens of different states.

3 Representative

Representatives can make laws, declare war, coin and print

money, control commerce, and raise an army and a navy.

CALIFORNIA STANDARDS HSS 5.7, 5.7.4   Use after reading Chapter 10, Lesson 3, pages 434–439.   Homework and Practice Book ▪ 103

© Harcourt

Skills: Read a Flowchart

DIRECTIONS Use the flowchart to help you answer the questions on the next page.

Presidential Elections

State Primary Elections
Some states hold primary elections. Voters in each major party choose which candidate for President they support.

State Conventions
Some political parties hold state conventions. There, delegates decide which candidate to support for President.

National Conventions
The summer before the election, each major political party holds a national convention. Delegates from all the states vote to choose the party's candidates for President and Vice President.

Election Day
On the first Tuesday after the first Monday in November, voters cast their ballots. This is called the popular vote.

Electoral Vote
In December, electors meet in each state to pledge their votes for the candidate who won the popular vote. They almost always vote for the candidate who won the popular vote, but they are not required to do so. The electors send the results of their vote to the president of the Senate.

Electoral Count
The president of the Senate counts the electoral votes from all states and announces the winner of the election.

Inauguration
The newly elected President and Vice President take office in a ceremony held on January 20.

(continued)

CALIFORNIA STANDARDS HSS 5.7, 5.7.3   Use after reading Chapter 10, Skill Lesson, pages 440–441.

© Harcourt

Name _____ Date _____

Approval and the Bill of Rights

DIRECTIONS Complete the diagram to show the freedoms guaranteed by the First Amendment.

- freedom of religion
- freedom of the press
- First Amendment
- freedom to petition the government for a redress of grievances
- freedom of speech
- freedom of assembly

DIRECTIONS Write a sentence telling one way in which people today express one of these freedoms.

Possible response: **People express freedom of the press by publishing newspapers.**

CALIFORNIA STANDARDS HSS 5.7, 5.7.4   Use after reading Chapter 10, Lesson 4, pages 442–447.

(continued)

Name _____ Date _____

1. What step comes before Election Day?
   The parties hold national conventions to choose their candidates.

2. Does the electoral vote happen before or after the popular vote?
   after

3. What is the last step in a presidential election?
   inauguration

4. Who counts the electoral votes?
   the president of the Senate

5. Which two parts of the process happen before the national conventions?
   state primary elections and state conventions

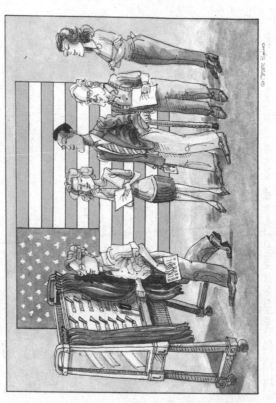

Use after reading Chapter 10, Skill Lesson, pages 440–441.   Homework and Practice Book ■ 105

Name _____ Date _____

Study Guide

Chapter 10

DIRECTIONS Fill in the missing information in these paragraphs about the Constitution. Use the terms below to help you complete the paragraphs.

Lesson 1	Lesson 2	Lesson 3	Lesson 4
convention	compromise	impeach	Alexander Hamilton
Daniel Shays	republic	veto	Thomas Jefferson
James Madison	federal system	amendments	John Adams
Patrick Henry		justices	
arsenal			

Lesson 1   In 1787, ___Daniel Shays___ and other protesters tried to

take over a government ___arsenal___ in Massachusetts. The

government had no army to defend its property. This persuaded many leaders

that the nation needed a stronger government. ___James Madison___

wanted to replace the Articles of Confederation. Other leaders, including

___Patrick Henry___, wanted to keep the Articles as they were. Still,

12 states sent delegates to a ___convention___ in Philadelphia. Its

purpose was to fix the Articles of Confederation.

CALIFORNIA STANDARDS HSS 5.7, 5.7.1, 5.7.2, 5.7.3, 5.7.4   Use after reading Chapter 10, pages 420–449.

108 ■ Homework and Practice Book

© Harcourt

Name _____ Date _____

DIRECTIONS Next to each number, write the letter of the correct description.

Bill of Rights

f ① Second Amendment

c ② Third Amendment

d ③ Fourth Amendment

a ④ Fifth Amendment, Sixth Amendment, Seventh Amendment, Eighth Amendment

e ⑤ Ninth Amendment

b ⑥ Tenth Amendment

a. Due process of law is guaranteed.

b. The national government can do only the things listed in the Constitution.

c. People cannot be forced to provide housing for soldiers in peacetime.

d. People's homes cannot be searched without a good reason.

e. People have other rights besides the ones listed in the Constitution.

f. It protects people's right to have weapons.

Use after reading Chapter 10, Lesson 4, pages 442–447.   Homework and Practice Book ■ 107

© Harcourt

54 ■ Homework and Practice Book Teacher Edition

READING SOCIAL STUDIES: DRAW CONCLUSIONS

The Constitutional Convention

DIRECTIONS Complete this graphic organizer to show that you can draw conclusions about the Constitutional Convention.

Evidence
The discussions at the Constitutional Convention were kept secret.

Knowledge
People keep things secret when they do not want others to interfere in what they are doing.

Conclusion
The delegates at the Constitutional Convention did not want others to influence their decisions.

Evidence
Delegates who supported the Constitution needed nine states to approve it.

Knowledge
People sometimes have to compromise to get what they want.

Conclusion
To win approval for the Constitution, delegates who supported it had to compromise.

CALIFORNIA STANDARDS HSS 5.7, 5.7.2

Use after reading Chapter 10, pages 420–449.

Lesson 2 Delegates to the Constitutional Convention had to **compromise** to settle their disagreements. Many of these disagreements were about government powers. The delegates finally agreed to strengthen the existing **federal system**, in which power was shared by the national government and the state governments. The government that the delegates created was a **republic** _____, in which people choose representatives to run the government.

Lesson 3 Under the Constitution, each branch of government limits the power of the other branches. For example, the President can **veto** _____, or reject, bills that Congress passes. Congress can **impeach** the President. The President nominates Supreme Court **justices** _____, but the Senate must approve them. The Constitution also explains the process for adding **amendments** _____, or changes.

Lesson 4 Disagreements among the nation's leaders led to the first political parties. **Alexander Hamilton** was a leader of the Federalists, who wanted a strong federal government. **Thomas Jefferson** was an Anti-Federalist who helped form the Democratic-Republican Party. In 1796, the Federalist candidate, **John Adams** _____, became the nation's second President.

Use after reading Chapter 10, pages 420–449.

Name _____ Date _____

Skills: Read a Population Map

DIRECTIONS Use the map to help you answer the questions.

United States Population Density

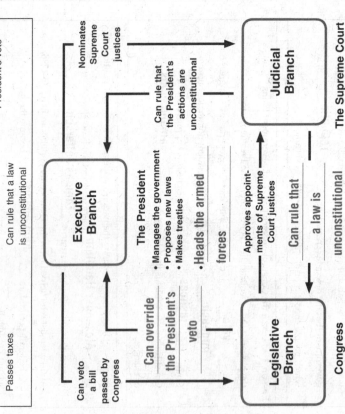

Persons per square mile
- More than 500
- 250–500
- 50–250
- 10–50
- Fewer than 10

CALIFORNIA STANDARDS HSS 5.7, 5.7.3; CS 4   Use after reading Chapter 11, Skill Lesson, pages 464–465.

(continued)

© Harcourt

Name _____ Date _____

A Constitutional Democracy

DIRECTIONS Use the phrases in the box to complete the chart. The arrows show how one branch of the government can affect another.

Heads the armed forces	Can override the President's veto
Approves treaties	
Passes taxes	Can rule that a law is unconstitutional

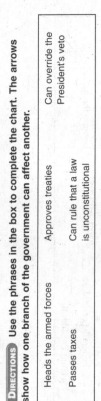

Executive Branch

The President
- Manages the government
- Proposes new laws
- Makes treaties
- **Heads the armed forces**

Can veto a bill passed by Congress

Can override the President's veto

Nominates Supreme Court justices

Can rule that the President's actions are unconstitutional

Judicial Branch

The Supreme Court and Other Federal Courts
- Decide whether or not laws are constitutional
- Explain the meanings of treaties

Can rule that a law is unconstitutional

Approves appointments of Supreme Court justices

Legislative Branch

Congress
- Passes taxes
- Makes laws
- **Approves treaties**
- Approves appointments

CALIFORNIA STANDARDS HSS 5.7, 5.7.3   Use after reading Chapter 11, Lesson 1, pages 458–463.   Homework and Practice Book ■ 111

© Harcourt

Name _____ Date _____

1 Which is more densely populated, the area around Burlington or the area around Charlotte? **the area around Charlotte**

2 What is the population density of the area in which Virginia Beach is located? **10–50 per square mile**

3 What is the population density in the United States of most of the area bordering Mexico? **fewer than 10 per square mile**

4 What are the most densely populated parts of California? **areas around cities on the south and central coasts—Los Angeles, San Francisco, and San Diego**

5 Which part of the country has the higher population density, the East or the West? **the East**

6 Which region of the country has the higher population density, the Great Lakes region or the Pacific Northwest region? **the Great Lakes region**

7 Which state has the lowest population density? **Alaska**

8 What is the population density where you live? Place an "X" on the map to mark the location.

9 What is the population density of the area surrounding where you live? _____ Place a circle around the "X" to mark this area.

Name _____ Date _____

American Ideals

DIRECTIONS Read the following verse of "America the Beautiful." Then answer the questions.

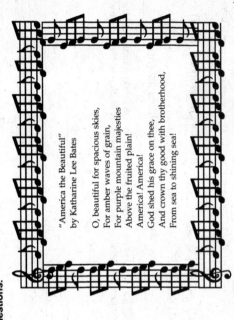

"America the Beautiful"
by Katharine Lee Bates

O, beautiful for spacious skies,
For amber waves of grain,
For purple mountain majesties
Above the fruited plain!
America! America!
God shed his grace on thee,
And crown thy good with brotherhood,
From sea to shining sea!

1 What landforms does the song mention? **mountains and plains**

2 What do the phrases "waves of grain" and "the fruited plain" tell you about America, besides that it is beautiful? **They describe a country where food is plentiful.**

3 What does the phrase "from sea to shining sea" refer to? **It refers to the area from the Atlantic Ocean to the Pacific Ocean.**

4 What is one American ideal that the song reflects? **Possible responses: brotherhood, or unity; patriotism, or love of country**

5 Write a sentence telling how you feel or what you think of when you read the words to this song. **Possible response: It reminds me that the United States is beautiful.**

CALIFORNIA STANDARDS HSS 5.7, 5.7.6

Name _____ Date _____

Preserving the Constitution

DIRECTIONS Read the statements below. Then choose the term from the box that best relates to each statement below.

| Americans with Disabilities Act (ADA) | American Indian Movement (AIM) |
| United Farm Workers (UFW) | naturalization | civil rights |

1 "I had to go through this process in order to become a
United States Citizen." **naturalization**

2 "I believe in Martin Luther King's dream of equal treat-
ment for all citizens under the law." **civil rights**

3 "I was inspired by the African American Civil Rights
Movement to begin working for the rights of the Sioux
people." **American Indian Movement (AIM)**

4 "My parents worked for grape growers in California
for low pay until Cesar Chavez and others organized a
United Farm Workers (UFW)

boycott to gain better wages."

5 "This law makes it easier for me to get a job based on my ability to perform
the job." **Americans with Disabilities Act (ADA)**

DIRECTIONS Choose an American leader who has worked to uphold the
Constitution, and briefly describe his or her contribution to the country.

_____

_____

_____

_____

CALIFORNIA STANDARDS HSS 5.7, 5.7.5   Use after reading Chapter 11, Lesson 3, pages 474–478.

© Harcourt

Name _____ Date _____

Skills: Read an Editorial Cartoon

DIRECTIONS Read the paragraph below, and then look carefully at the editorial
cartoon. Read the labels. Then answer the questions.

This cartoon uses pillars, or columns, to represent the states involved in building
the federal system of government. Those pillars that stand side by side represent
states that have already agreed to ratify the Constitution. The last two pillars
represent North Carolina and Rhode Island.

1 What do the pillars in the cartoon represent? **the 13 original states**

2 What could the pillars standing together be a symbol of? **strength**

3 Why are the last two pillars leaning? **Possible responses: They are not
strong enough to stand on their own. They have not yet agreed
to ratify the Constitution.**

4 What were the last two states to ratify the Constitution?
North Carolina and Rhode Island

5 What does the cartoon express about the federal system?
The federal system gives the states greater strength.

CALIFORNIA STANDARDS HSS 5.7, 5.7.2   Use after reading Chapter 11, Skill Lesson, pages 470–471.   Homework and Practice Book ■ 115

© Harcourt

Name _____ Date _____

Skills: Act as a Responsible Citizen

DIRECTIONS Read each statement below. Then suggest how you might act as a responsible citizen to handle the situation.

1. You notice that people are being careless about litter in your neighborhood. **Possible response: I could organize a group to monitor litter or petition for more trash containers to be placed in public areas.**

2. At a park, you see a dog that seems to be a stray. **Possible response: I could contact a local animal shelter.**

3. Skateboarders in your neighborhood are practicing on sidewalks and in the street. **Possible response: I could write a letter to local leaders, asking them to designate a skateboard park area.**

4. A local election is coming up. **Possible response: I could learn about the candidates who are running for office and find out what they propose to do if they are elected.**

5. A new law has been proposed and will soon be voted on. Some people do not like the new law. **Possible response: I could ask the mayor or city council to hold a meeting at which people could express their opinions of the law.**

CALIFORNIA STANDARDS HSS 5.7, 5.7.5

Use after reading Chapter 11, Skill Lesson, pages 480–481.   Homework and Practice Book ■ 117

Name _____ Date _____

Study Guide

DIRECTIONS Fill in the missing information in these paragraphs about the American government and the roles of citizens. Use the terms below to help you complete the paragraphs.

Lesson 1	Lesson 2	Lesson 3
declare war	patriotism	Justin Dart
collect taxes	Francis Scott Key	civil rights
create an army	Mary Pickersgill	Earl Warren
set up public schools	ideals	Martin Luther King, Jr.
conduct elections	creed	Cesar Chavez

Lesson 1 In the federal system of government, the national government and the state governments each have powers and responsibilities. Only the national government can **declare war**. Only state governments can **create an army** and **conduct elections**. **set up public schools** and **collect taxes**. Both the national government and state governments can

CALIFORNIA STANDARDS HSS 5.7, 5.7.3, 5.7.4, 5.7.5, 5.7.6

Use after reading Chapter 11, pages 458–481.

118 ■ Homework and Practice Book

(continued)

Homework and Practice Book Teacher Edition ■ 59

READING SOCIAL STUDIES: DRAW CONCLUSIONS

Working for Equality

DIRECTIONS Complete this graphic organizer to show that you can draw conclusions about how people worked to preserve American ideals.

Evidence
In 1963, more than 250,000 people marched for civil rights.

→

Knowledge
Calling attention to injustice often helps bring change.

Conclusion
About a year after the march in Washington, Congress passed the Civil Rights Act of 1964.

Evidence
In the past, many Americans were denied the right to vote.

→

Knowledge
Laws can be changed to extend freedoms to more people.

Conclusion
In 1965, Congress passed a law to make sure that all Americans can vote in elections.

CALIFORNIA STANDARDS HSS 5.7, 5.7.5

Use after reading Chapter 11, pages 458–481.

Lesson 2 The principles of freedom, equality, and justice are at the heart of the American **creed** , or system of beliefs. These principles are **ideals** , or goals, that Americans work to put into practice. Some well-known symbols and songs are reminders of these goals. One important national symbol is the American flag. **Mary Pickersgill** made the flag that inspired what later became the national anthem. Our national anthem, "The Star-Spangled Banner," is a song of **patriotism** . It was written by **Francis Scott Key** .

Lesson 3 Many Americans have worked to make sure that the **civil rights** of all Americans are protected. **Martin Luther King, Jr.** , showed African Americans how to use nonviolent means to win their rights. Under former Chief Justice **Earl Warren** , the Supreme Court made decisions that upheld these rights. **Cesar Chavez** worked to improve the lives of migrant farm workers. **Justin Dart** helped get a law passed that protects the rights of disabled persons.

© Harcourt

Name _____ Date _____

Skills: Compare Graphs

DIRECTIONS Compare the graphs below to help you answer the questions on the next page.

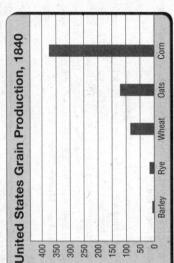

Origin of Immigrants to the United States, 1820–1840

Europe 80%

Africa* 14%

The Americas 6%

*and other regions, excluding Asia

Immigration to the United States, 1832–1840

Number of People (in thousands)

90
80
70
60
50
40
30
20
10
0

1832 1834 1836 1838 1840

Year

United States Grain Production, 1840

Millions of Bushels

400
350
300
250
200
150
100
50
0

Barley Rye Wheat Oats Corn

CALIFORNIA STANDARDS HSS 5.8, 5.8.1; CS 1   Use after reading Chapter 12, Skill Lesson, pages 506–507.

(continued)

© Harcourt

Name _____ Date _____

A Growing Population

DIRECTIONS Use the map to help you answer the questions.

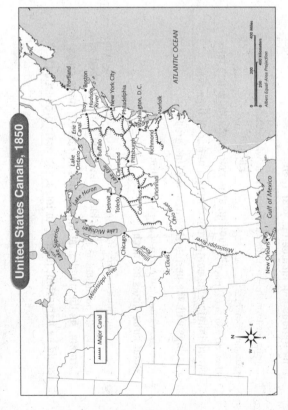

United States Canals, 1850

Major Canal

Portland
Boston
Troy
Erie Canal
Hudson River
New York City
Philadelphia
Washington, D.C.
Richmond
Norfolk
Buffalo
Lake Ontario
Lake Erie
Cleveland
Cincinnati
Columbus
Detroit
Toledo
Lake Michigan
Lake Huron
Lake Superior
Chicago
Illinois River
Ohio River
Mississippi River
St. Louis
New Orleans
Gulf of Mexico

ATLANTIC OCEAN

N E S W

0   200   400 Miles
0   200   400 Kilometers
Albers Equal-Area Projection

① What two natural waterways did the Erie Canal connect?
Lake Erie and the Hudson River

② What two cities did it connect?   **Buffalo and Troy**

③ What are two other natural waterways that were connected by canals?
Possible response: Lake Michigan and the Illinois River

④ What are two other cities that were connected by canals?
Possible response: Pittsburgh and Philadelphia

⑤ Through what city did the southernmost canal run?   **Richmond**

CALIFORNIA STANDARDS HSS 5.8, 5.8.1

Use after reading Chapter 12, Lesson 1, pages 500–505.   Homework and Practice Book ■ 121

© Harcourt

Homework and Practice Book Teacher Edition ■ 61

Name _____ Date _____

Pioneer Life

DIRECTIONS Using pages 509 and 510 in your textbook, complete the web diagram to tell about pioneer life.

Early pioneers crossed the Appalachian Mountains, drawn west by a land rich in natural resources. They found a landscape made up of thick forests, broad rivers, and streams. They cut down trees and used them to make shelters. After building a new home, a pioneer family began clearing fields for crops. The family dug up the earth and planted seeds in the rich soil. Some pioneers used water from nearby streams to water their fields. If all went well, the mild climate and the long growing season would bring the pioneers a good harvest.

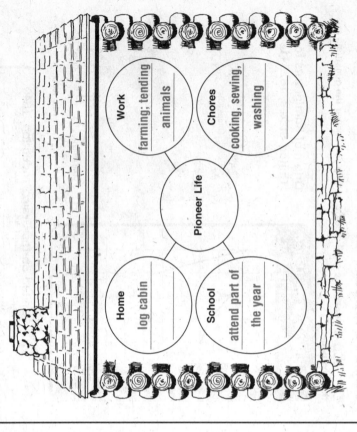

Web diagram — **Pioneer Life** (center), connected to:
- **Work:** farming; tending animals
- **Chores:** cooking, sewing, washing
- **Home:** log cabin
- **School:** attend part of the year

(continued)

Name _____ Date _____

1. Which kind of graph shows the number of immigrants who came to the United States in 1840? **the line graph**

2. Which kind of graph shows what percentage of immigrants came from Europe in one 20-year period? **the circle graph**

3. Which kind of graph best shows change over time? **the line graph**

4. How do the time periods shown on the three graphs compare? **The longer time period shown on the circle graph includes the period shown on the line graph. The bar graph shows data for the year 1840 only, while the other two graphs cover longer time periods that include the year 1840.**

5. During the time shown on the line graph, from where did most immigrants probably come? **Europe**

6. How do you know this? **by looking at the circle graph, which tells where immigrants came from during a period of time that overlaps with the period shown on the line graph**

7. About how much more corn was produced than oats? **about three times as much**

8. How do you think the arrival of immigrants in the United States might have affected grain production in 1840? **Many new immigrants worked as farmers. As the number of immigrants increased, more crops could be harvested, leading to increased grain production.**

© Harcourt

Name _____
Date _____

DIRECTIONS Read each statement. On the line provided, write the name of the person the statement describes.

Mike Fink	Paul Bunyan
John Chapman	Abraham Lincoln
Daniel Drake	

1 From the time he was 8 years old, he worked alongside his father on their Kentucky farm. **Daniel Drake**

2 He was a sailor on the Mississippi River, and people said he wrestled alligators. **Mike Fink**

3 He traveled through Pennsylvania, Ohio, Indiana, and Illinois, planting trees. **John Chapman**

4 He was a favorite character in tall tales, and one popular song claimed that he stood thirty-five feet tall. **Paul Bunyan**

5 He went from a frontier shelter made of branches and logs to the White House. **Abraham Lincoln**

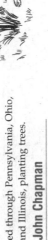

Name _____
Date _____

Exploring the West

DIRECTIONS Below is a fictional letter from a member of the Corps of Discovery to a friend back home. Use the words and phrases in the box to complete the letter.

Rocky Mountains	Meriwether Lewis	North Dakota
Sacagawea	Thomas Jefferson	St. Louis
Pacific Ocean	William Clark	horses
Fort Mandan		

Dear Robert:

Wonderful news! We have begun our journey home, and we hope to return to **St. Louis** before autumn.

After we left there, we spent the winter of 1804–1805 in **North Dakota**. We built a camp and named it **Fort Mandan**, after the Indians who lived nearby.

In this same place, we met a Shoshone Indian woman who helped us greatly. Her name was **Sacagawea**, and she guided us safely through the lands of her people. She helped us buy **horses**, which we used to cross the **Rocky Mountains**. Then we built boats and rowed down several rivers, including the Columbia River. In November 1805, we finally reached the **Pacific Ocean**.

Our expedition succeeded because of our skilled leaders, **Meriwether Lewis** and **William Clark**. They made maps of our journey and also collected seeds, plants, and animals to show **Thomas Jefferson**. I know he will be glad that he persuaded Congress to pay for our trip.

I am eager to see you and hear your news.

Yours truly,

John

CALIFORNIA STANDARDS HSS 5.8, 5.8.3

Skills: Make a Thoughtful Decision

Name _____ Date _____

DIRECTIONS Imagine you are leading an expedition that is looking for a route to the Pacific Coast. You want to travel west by river, but you do not know this river well. Follow the steps below to decide on a course of action.

Step 1 *Make a list of choices you could make to help you reach your goal.*

1 I could try to lead the expedition upriver.

2 I could turn back and try to find another route west.

Step 2 *Gather information you will need to make a good decision.*

3 Possible response: I will watch to see if there are other boats traveling the river.

4 Possible response: I will send scouts upriver to take measurements of the river's current and depth.

5 Possible response: I will check to make sure that we have the supplies that we will need to make rafts.

Step 3 *Predict consequences, and compare them.*

6 Possible response: If the river is too difficult to travel, we will have wasted time building rafts and trying to travel it.

7 Possible response: If we turn back, we will be moving away from the Pacific Coast, which is our goal.

Step 4 *Make a choice, and take action.*

8 Possible response: I will try to take the expedition upriver. I gave the order to start building rafts.

Tell why you made the choice you made.

9 Possible response: I want to lead the expedition toward its goal.

📖 **CALIFORNIA STANDARDS HSS 5.8, 5.8.3**

Use after reading Chapter 12, Skill Lesson, pages 520–521.   Homework and Practice Book ▪ 127

© Harcourt

The War of 1812

Name _____ Date _____

DIRECTIONS Look at the time line below. Match each event with the correct date on the time line. Write the correct letter of the event in the blank provided.

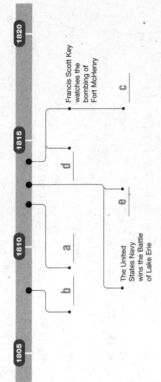

Francis Scott Key watches the bombing of Fort McHenry — c

The United States Navy wins the Battle of Lake Erie

1805   1810   1815   1820

b   a   d   e   c

Tecumseh

a ___ The United States declares war on Britain

b ___ Chief Tecumseh and his brother establish Prophetstown, where they hope to unite Indians to fight the United States Army

c ___ The United States and Britain sign a peace treaty

d ___ British troops capture Washington, D.C., and burn the White House

e ___ American troops win the Battle of the Thames; Chief Tecumseh is killed

📖 **CALIFORNIA STANDARDS HSS 5.3, 5.3.6; CS 1**   Use after reading Chapter 12, Lesson 4, pages 522–525.

128 ▪ Homework and Practice Book

American Indian Life Changes

DIRECTIONS Read the passage. Then answer the questions.

Nancy Ward, Cherokee Peacemaker

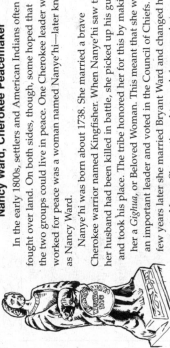

Statue of
Nancy Ward

In the early 1800s, settlers and American Indians often fought over land. On both sides, though, some hoped that the two groups could live in peace. One Cherokee leader who worked for peace was a woman named Nanye'hi—later known as Nancy Ward.

Nanye'hi was born about 1738. She married a brave Cherokee warrior named Kingfisher. When Nanye'hi saw that her husband had been killed in battle, she picked up his gun and took his place. The tribe honored her for this by making her a *Gighua*, or Beloved Woman. This meant that she was an important leader and voted in the Council of Chiefs. A few years later she married Bryant Ward and changed her name to Nancy. She continued to work for peace between the settlers and the Cherokee.

In 1776, Nanye'hi warned settlers of a planned Indian attack. When a captured settler was brought to Nanye'hi's village, Nanye'hi insisted that the woman not be killed. Nanye'hi also negotiated peace treaties with the United States government. However, the government and the settlers often ignored peace treaties. They took more and more land from the Cherokee. In 1817, Nanye'hi told her people to fight the settlers if that was the only way they could keep their land. Two years later, Nanye'hi and other Cherokee in her area were forced off their land. They settled nearby to the south. She died in 1824, before the Cherokee were forced to follow the Trail of Tears to Oklahoma.

1. What was Nancy Ward's role in Cherokee government? **She was a leader who voted in the Council of Chiefs.**

2. How did Nancy Ward try to keep peace between the Cherokee and settlers? **She negotiated treaties and warned settlers of Indian attacks.**

3. Why did Nancy Ward finally tell the Cherokee to fight the settlers? **The settlers took more and more Cherokee land.**

Chapter 12 Study Guide

DIRECTIONS Fill in the missing information in these paragraphs about frontier life. Use the terms below to help you complete the paragraphs.

Lesson 1	Lesson 2	Lesson 3	Lesson 4	Lesson 5
canals	Kentucky	Sacagawea	Tecumseh	Sequoyah
flatboats	Tennessee	York	James Madison	John Ross
locks	Vermont	William Clark	encroached	Osceola
pathfinders			Francis Scott Key	

Lesson 1 As Americans moved farther west, they followed routes found by earlier **pathfinders** . They used waterways to travel to new homes and to transport goods. At first, large rafts called **flatboats** were floated down rivers. Later, steam-boats made traveling upstream easier and faster. In the early 1800s, Americans dug **canals** to connect natural waterways. **Locks** were used to raise and lower boats at places where water levels differed.

Lesson 2 The first state added to the original 13 states was **Vermont** . In the next year, 1792, **Kentucky** became the first state west of the Appalachian Mountains. It got its name from an Iroquois word meaning "land of tomorrow." In 1796, **Tennessee** , named after a Cherokee village, also became a state.

🐾 **CALIFORNIA STANDARDS HSS 5.3, 5.3.4, 5.3.6, 5.8, 5.8.1, 5.8.2, 5.8.3, 5.8.4**

130 ▪ Homework and Practice Book   Use after reading Chapter 12, pages 500–533.

(continued)

READING SOCIAL STUDIES: GENERALIZE

(Focus Skill) Living on the Frontier

DIRECTIONS Complete this graphic organizer to show that you can make generalizations about life on the frontier during the early 1800s.

Facts

Land was cheap and plentiful.	The climate was good for growing crops.	The soil was fertile.

➡

Generalization

Most frontier families lived on farms.

Facts

Cabins and shelters had to be built.	Chores could take all day long.	Children began working at a very young age.

➡

Generalization

Living on the frontier involved hard work.

CALIFORNIA STANDARDS HSS 5.8, 5.8.4

Use after reading Chapter 12, pages 501–533.

Lesson 3 In 1804, the Corps of Discovery set out to explore Louisiana. The leaders of the expedition were Meriwether Lewis and __William Clark__. Among the 30 or so adventurers was a slave named __York__ who was a skilled hunter and fisher. __Sacagawea__ guided the men through Shoshone lands.

Lesson 4 One cause of the War of 1812 was settlers who __encroached__ on Indian lands. The Shawnee Chief __Tecumseh__ tried to unite Indians to fight the settlers. British soldiers allied with the Indians. __James Madison__ asked Congress to declare war on Britain in 1812. In 1814, the British sailed to Baltimore, where __Francis Scott Key__ watched British ships bomb Fort McHenry. The poem he wrote about the event later became the national anthem.

Lesson 5 In the early 1800s, Indian leaders tried to defend their lands and peoples from settlers. The Seminole Chief __Osceola__ led attacks on American soldiers in the Florida swamps. __Sequoyah__ helped preserve the Cherokee language. Chief __John Ross__, also a Cherokee, won a victory for his people in the United States Supreme Court. However, President Andrew Jackson refused to enforce the court's decision. As a result, the Cherokee lost their lands in the East.

Use after reading Chapter 12, pages 500–533.

© Harcourt

Western Trails

DIRECTIONS Follow the instructions below to complete the map.

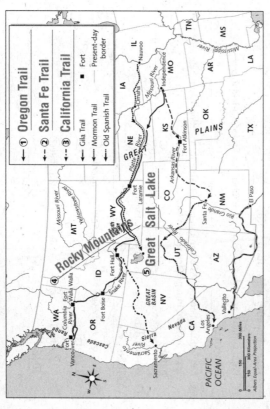

Legend:
① Oregon Trail
② Santa Fe Trail
③ California Trail
Gila Trail
Mormon Trail
Old Spanish Trail
■ Fort
Present-day border

1. In the legend, write the name of the trail that began at Independence, Missouri, and led northwest.

2. In the legend, write the name of the trail that began at Independence, Missouri, and led southwest.

3. In the legend, write the name of the trail that connected Fort Hall and Sacramento.

4. On the map, write the name of the large mountain range that the trails crossed.

5. On the map, write the name of the lake where the Mormon Trail ended.

CALIFORNIA STANDARDS HSS 5.8, 5.8.4

Use after reading Chapter 13, Lesson 1, pages 540–547.　　　Homework and Practice Book ■ 133

(continued)

DIRECTIONS Use the completed map to help you answer the questions.

1. Which trail began at the Mississippi River? **the Mormon Trail**

2. Which trail crossed the Arkansas River? **the Santa Fe Trail**

3. What was the end point of the Oregon Trail? **Fort Vancouver**

4. What mountain range did the California Trail cross? **the Sierra Nevada**

5. Which trails ended in California? **the California Trail, the Gila Trail, the Old Spanish Trail**

6. Which trail passed the most forts? How many forts were there along this trail? **the Oregon Trail; five**

7. What fort was the farthest west? **Fort Vancouver**

8. Besides the names given for them on the map, how can you tell where the forts are located? **The legend shows that a fort is represented on the map by a black square.**

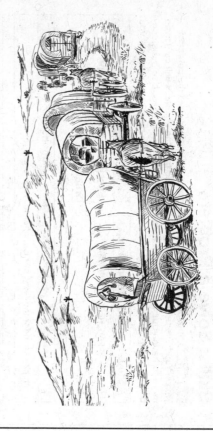

A Growing Nation

Name _____ Date _____

DIRECTIONS Use the time line to help you answer the questions below.

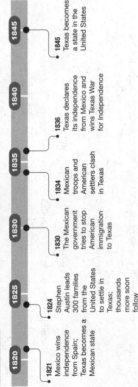

1821 Mexico wins independence from Spain; Texas becomes a Mexican state

1824 Stephen Austin leads 300 families from the United States to settle in Texas; thousands more soon follow

1830 The Mexican government tries to stop American immigration to Texas

1834 Mexican troops and American settlers clash in Texas

1836 Texas declares its independence from Mexico and wins Texas War for Independence

1845 Texas becomes a state in the United States

1. When Mexico won independence from Spain in 1821, what did Texas become?
   Texas became a Mexican state.

2. What country governed Texas when Stephen Austin led settlers there?
   Mexico

3. Did fighting between Mexican troops and American settlers begin before or after Texas declared independence from Mexico?
   before

4. When did the Texas War for Independence end?
   1836

5. For how many years was Texas an independent republic?
   9 years

6. When did Texas become a state in the United States?
   1845

CALIFORNIA STANDARDS HSS 5.8, 5.8.6

Use after reading Chapter 13, Lesson 2, pages 550–554.   Homework and Practice Book ■ 135

© Harcourt

Skills: Solve a Problem

Name _____ Date _____

DIRECTIONS Imagine that, after a long journey, you have reached the border of Texas. You have used a lot of money and supplies to come this far. It will cost even more to have your wagon ferried across the Red River to Texas. Use the steps below to help you solve the problem. Three of the steps have been done for you.

Step 1: Identify the problem.
I have to get my wagon across the Red River.

Step 2: Gather information.
Possible response: I found out what the ferry costs.

Step 3: List possible solutions.
I can pay cash for the ferry, or I can offer to work to pay for it.

Step 4: Consider the advantages and disadvantages of each solution.
Possible response: If I pay cash then I can now cross. If I offer to work, I can save money, but I will run even lower on supplies.

Step 5: Choose the best solution.
Possible response: I chose to pay cash for the ferry because I need to get to Texas to replenish my supplies and to start my new farm.

Step 6: Try your solution.
Imagine yourself applying the solution you chose. Think through what might happen and what the results might be.

Step 7: Tell about how well your solution helped solve the problem.
Possible response: I was able to achieve my goal, even though I may have to work to overcome the disadvantages of my choice.

CALIFORNIA STANDARDS HSS 5.8, 5.8.4   Use after reading Chapter 13, Skill Lesson, pages 556–557.

136 ■ Homework and Practice Book

© Harcourt

Name _____   Date _____

From Ocean to Ocean

DIRECTIONS Next to each name of each person, write the letter of the description that tells about that person.

1 d James K. Polk

2 c Mariano Vallejo

3 b John Sutter

4 e James Buchanan

5 f Zachary Taylor

6 a James Gadsden

a. arranged for the United States to buy land from Mexico

b. owned the land where gold was first discovered in California

c. worked for California statehood

d. expanded United States territory both to the north and to the south

e. signed the bill making Oregon a state

f. gave orders to have a fort built on land Mexico had claimed

DIRECTIONS Imagine that you have been asked to write an interview for a local newspaper. On a separate sheet of paper, write three questions that you would ask during an interview with one of the individuals listed above.

CALIFORNIA STANDARDS HSS 5.8, 5.8.6

Use after reading Chapter 13, Lesson 3, pages 558–564.   Homework and Practice Book ■ 137

Name _____   Date _____

Skills: Identify Changing Borders

DIRECTIONS Use the map to help you answer the questions.

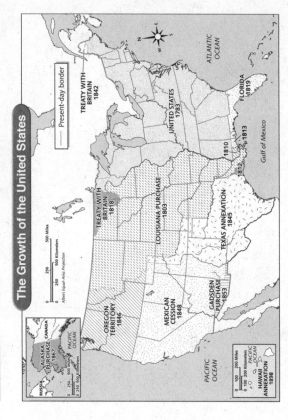

The Growth of the United States

1 In what year did the United States add the most new territory? **1803**

2 What was the last territory added to the United States? **Hawaii**

3 What present-day state became part of the United States in 1845? **Texas**

4 In what year did California become part of the United States? **1848**

5 What generalization can you make about the direction of the growth of the United States? **It grew westward.**

CALIFORNIA STANDARDS HSS 5.8, 5.8.2, 5.8.6; CS 4   Use after reading Chapter 13, Skill Lesson, pages 566–567.

138 ■ Homework and Practice Book

Name _____ Date _____

Skills: Read a Time Zone Map

DIRECTIONS Use the map below to help you answer the questions on page 141.

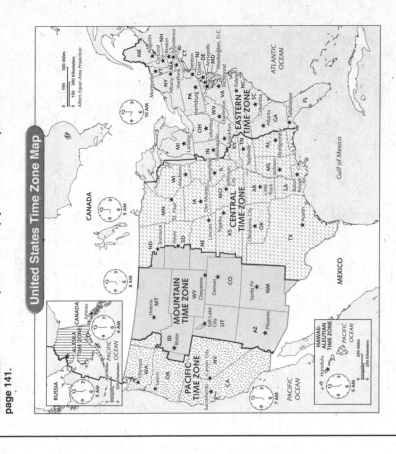

United States Time Zone Map

(continued)

CALIFORNIA STANDARDS HSS 5.9; CS 4   Use after reading Chapter 13, Skill Lesson, pages 576–577.

140 ■ Homework and Practice Book

© Harcourt

Name _____ Date _____

New People and New Ideas

DIRECTIONS Complete the graphic organizer to show how new people and new inventions changed life in the United States.

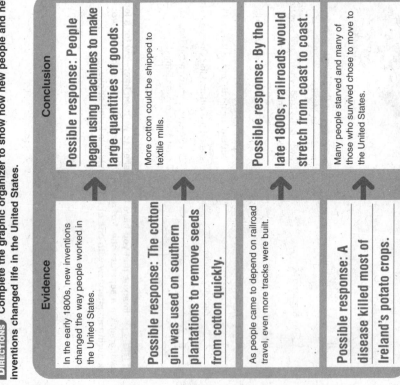

Evidence	Conclusion
In the early 1800s, new inventions changed the way people worked in the United States.	**Possible response: People began using machines to make large quantities of goods.**
Possible response: The cotton gin was used on southern plantations to remove seeds from cotton quickly.	More cotton could be shipped to textile mills.
As people came to depend on railroad travel, even more tracks were built.	**Possible response: By the late 1800s, railroads would stretch from coast to coast.**
Possible response: A disease killed most of Ireland's potato crops.	Many people starved and many of those who survived chose to move to the United States.

CALIFORNIA STANDARDS HSS 5.8, 5.8.2   Use after reading Chapter 13, Lesson 4, pages 568–574.   Homework and Practice Book ■ 139

© Harcourt

Name _____ Date _____

1. What is the capital of California, and what time zone is it in?
   Sacramento; the Pacific time zone

2. What two time zones cover Texas?
   the Central time zone and the Mountain time zone

3. Which time zone is the capital of Texas in?
   the Central time zone

4. If it is noon in the capital of Florida, what time is it in the capital of Oregon?
   9 A.M.

5. How much time difference is there between California and Hawaii?
   2 hours

6. How much time difference is there between the capital of Illinois and the capital of Colorado?
   1 hour

7. Which of these capitals is in the Eastern time zone: Indianapolis, Springfield, Jefferson City?
   Indianapolis

8. What time zone is the capital of New Mexico in?
   the Mountain time zone

9. What time zone is most of the Great Lakes region in?
   the Eastern time zone

10. When it is 9 A.M. in the capital of Nevada, what time is it in the capital of New York?
    noon

Chapter 13

Name _____ Date _____

Study Guide

DIRECTIONS Fill in the missing information in these paragraphs about the westward growth of the United States. Use the terms below to help you complete the paragraphs.

Lesson 1	Lesson 2	Lesson 3	Lesson 4
William Becknell	slave state	gold rush	telegraph
Brigham Young	free state	manifest destiny	cotton gin
Narcissa Whitman	annex	forty-niners	interchangeable
Jedediah Smith		cession	parts
John C. Frémont			

Lesson 1 In the mid-1800s, thousands of settlers followed trails to the West. Pathfinders opened the way for them. Indians helped the trapper **Jedediah Smith** find a pass through the Rocky Mountains. **John C. Frémont** mapped the Oregon Trail. This map, along with letters written by the missionary **Narcissa Whitman**, drew settlers to Oregon. The Missouri trader **William Becknell** opened the Santa Fe Trail, which began in Independence, Missouri. **Brigham Young** led the first group of settlers along the Mormon Trail to the Great Salt Lake.

CALIFORNIA STANDARDS HSS 5.8, 5.8.4, 5.8.5, 5.8.6   Use after reading Chapter 13, pages 540–577.

(continued)

Name _____ Date _____

Lesson 2 The Mexican government encouraged Mexican settlers to migrate to lands that came to be known as Texas. Later, when Texans first voted to join the United States, the nation did not want to **annex** Texas. One reason was an argument over slavery. At least 30,000 slaves lived in Texas. Most Texans wanted Texas to join the union as a **slave state**. Americans who opposed slavery said that if Texas did not want to be a **free state** _____, it should not become a state at all.

Lesson 3 By the 1840s, the United States had expanded its territory all the way to the Pacific Ocean. This fulfilled the idea of **manifest destiny** _____. In 1846, the Oregon Treaty was signed, giving the Oregon Territory to the United States. In 1848, the United States got California, Nevada, Utah, and parts of other present-day states in a **cession** _____ from Mexico. At about the same time, a **gold rush** _____ brought thousands of settlers and immigrants to California. Many of these settlers were called **forty-niners** _____, after the year of their arrival.

Lesson 4 During the Industrial Revolution, machines were invented that could work faster than people could. For example, the **cotton gin** _____ could remove seeds much faster than human workers could. Another improvement was the invention of **interchangeable parts**, which allowed people to quickly repair machines that broke down. Machines even made communication faster. The **telegraph** _____ sent messages along wires over long distances.

© Harcourt

Name _____ Date _____

READING SOCIAL STUDIES: GENERALIZE

Focus Skill

Moving West

DIRECTIONS Complete this graphic organizer to show that you can make generalizations about the growth of the United States during the first half of the 1800s.

Facts

Settlers needed pathfinders to find safe trails and mountain passes.	Settlers had to carry enough water and supplies with them for the long journey.	Pioneers often waited until enough wagons had gathered to make a wagon train.

Generalization

Most people traveled west on wagon trails.

Facts

Workers at John Sutter's sawmill found gold in the American River.	Word slowly spread that there was gold in California.	Many people hoped to become rich by finding gold.

Generalization

People came to California from all over the world during the gold rush.

CALIFORNIA STANDARDS HSS 5.8, 5.8.4

© Harcourt